Essential Life Skills for Teens
The Ultimate Guide

Navigate Your Emotions, Build Relationships, Sharpen
Decision-Making, Improve Time Management,
Manage Finances and Unleash Your Greatness!

By Jordan Wize

CONTENTS

Introduction   7

1. UNDERSTANDING YOUR EMOTIONS:
   MASTER YOUR FEELINGS AND FOSTER
   POSITIVE RELATIONSHIPS   11
   A Sea of Emotions   11
   Exploring the World of Emotions   12
   Emotional Intelligence: The Key to
   Understanding and Managing Emotions   14
   Strategies for Managing Emotions   15

2. MAKING CENT$ OF YOUR DOLLAR: A TEEN'S
   GUIDE TO FINANCIAL LITERACY   25
   The ABCs of Money: Income, Expenses, and
   Savings   26
   Budgeting Basics: Creating Your Money Plan   27
   The ABCs of Bank Accounts - Checking and
   Savings   30
   Spending Wisely: Credit Cards and Making
   Smart Money Decisions   33
   Taxes and Insurance: Understanding the Basics   35
   Hands-On Financial Literacy: Practical Exercises   43

3. THE ART OF CONNECTION: BUILDING
   HEALTHY RELATIONSHIPS   49
   The Heart of the Matter: Different Types of
   Relationships   49
   Building Blocks: Elements of Healthy
   Relationships   53
   Navigating Choppy Waters: Managing Conflict
   in Relationships   56
   The Social Code: Understanding Social Etiquette   61

4. THE ART OF EXPRESSING YOURSELF   69
   Words Matter: Crafting Clear and Effective
   Verbal Communication   69
   Listening to Understand: The Power of Active
   Listening   71
   Silent Signals: Understanding Non-Verbal
   Communication   74
   Navigating Digital Communication: Social
   Media, Texting, and More   77
   Conflict Resolution: Communicating through
   Disagreements   79

5. CHARTING YOUR OWN PATH: THE ART OF
   INFORMED DECISION-MAKING   83
   The Power of Informed Decisions   83
   Unpacking the Decision-Making Process   85
   Overcoming Decision-Making Pressure   87
   Real-Life Scenarios to Practice Decision-Making
   Skills   89
   The Role of Values in Decision-Making   90

6. BECOMING A SOLUTION-FINDER: A TEEN'S
   GUIDE TO PROBLEM-SOLVING   97
   Understanding the Problem: The First Step to
   Finding Solutions   97
   Generating Solutions: The Power of
   Brainstorming   98
   Evaluating Options: Making the Right Choice   99
   Implementing the Solution: Turning Ideas into
   Action   102
   Reflecting on the Problem-Solving Process:
   Learning from Experience   103

7. BODY AND MIND: UNDERSTANDING
   PHYSICAL AND MENTAL HEALTH   107
   The Power of Good Nutrition   107
   Fitness First: The Role of Exercise   109
   Breaking Down the Basics of Mental Health   110
   Spotting Common Mental Health Problems
   among Teens   111
   Mastering Stress Management Techniques   114

Embracing the Power of Self-Care 116
Supporting Mental Health Online 118

8. NO PLACE LIKE HOME: MASTERING BASIC
LIFE SKILLS 123
Spin Cycle: Demystifying the Laundry Process 123
MasterChef Junior: Cooking Up Simple,
Nutritious Meals 127
Keep It Clean: Basic Housekeeping 101 128
Fresh and Clean: Personal Grooming and
Hygiene Practices 131

9. MASTERING TIME: MAKING EVERY MINUTE
COUNT 135
Time: The Most Valuable Currency 135
The Magic of Prioritizing 138
Maximizing Productivity with Tools and
Techniques 141
Tools for Efficiency 142
Keeping Procrastination at Bay 146
Mastering Time Management: Creating Life
Balance 148

10. SURFING THE DIGITAL WAVE: NAVIGATING
ONLINE LIFE 153
The Cyber Health Equation: Balancing
Screen Time 154
Digital Waves: Navigating Social Media and
Online Safety 155
Navigating the Power of AI 156
Digital Citizenship: Responsible Online Behavior 158
Nourishing Real Life: Balancing Digital and
Offline Worlds 159

11. CHARTING YOUR PATH: PLANNING YOUR
CAREER AND HUNTING FOR JOBS 163
Self-Exploration: Identifying Your Interests and
Skills 163
Career Exploration: Understanding Different
Career Paths 165
Crafting Your Resume: Making a Strong First
Impression 167

Preparing for Job Interviews: Showcasing Your
Skills and Enthusiasm   169
Understanding Workplace Etiquette: Navigating
Your First Job   171

Conclusion   177
References   181

INTRODUCTION

Just as a lighthouse stands unwavering against powerful ocean currents, guiding ships safely across sometimes treacherous waters, the life skills we are about to develop throughout this book will be your guiding light, helping you navigate the often unpredictable journey of your teenage years. Before we get started, with this bit of imagery in mind, I want us to embark on a slight adventure together as we bring this metaphor to life in the context of our work.

Imagine you are standing at the edge of the shoreline. As you look out on the vast expanse of the ocean, each wave is a challenge or an opportunity crashing towards you. Some swells are slow and gentle, quietly lapping at your feet. You feel calm and serene. Some waves, however, are violent. The sea churns with uncertainty and unexpected undertows that try to pull you out into the storm. Then, just as quickly, the waters quiet again. All is suddenly calm until the current boils up once more.

Now, picture a lighthouse standing proud on a distant, rocky shore. Its light is a beacon streaming through the darkness, offering guidance and direction to the sailors out at sea. You feel a sense of relief where before, there was none. Suddenly, you can see more clearly. There is a light shining onto your path.

The chapters in this book are like a lighthouse to a sailor. Whereas you may sometimes find yourself navigating a sea of mixed emotions, each chapter in this book is designed to serve as a beacon of light in the near distance of a stormy sea. Each chapter will provide you with an essential life skill, serving as your own lighthouses, illuminating adolescence's murky waters and helping you find your way as you make informed decisions about your future path.

Each chapter will cast a unique light on different aspects of your life that require development to become your best possible self. From understanding emotional regulation to learning appropriate time management techniques to keep your course consistent, each chapter will provide valuable insights to help weather the storms and seize the sunnier days.

Just as ocean currents challenge a ship's course throughout the day, obstacles and pressures will undoubtedly be a part of this journey toward self-discovery. But fear not! Each lighthouse will offer you a beacon of hope in what might otherwise be a dark night. Remember, you are at the helm of your ship, and with each chapter, you will steer your way through life's sea of emotions, newfound skills, and confidence. Let the lighthouse analogy be your companion, reminding you that no matter how stormy the waters, there is a light there to guide you as you steer onward toward tremendous growth.

And so, let the journey begin!

1

UNDERSTANDING YOUR EMOTIONS: MASTER YOUR FEELINGS AND FOSTER POSITIVE RELATIONSHIPS

A SEA OF EMOTIONS

As a teenager, you often sail upon waters like those mentioned in the introduction. In fact, as humans, we experience about 400 emotions on any given day, swirling around like the waves coming into shore. Sometimes, we encounter storms. Sometimes, the sea is calm. And most days, we experience several emotions throughout their course.

We all have emotions, but how well do we truly understand them? As teenagers, we experience many emotions simultaneously, meaning that we don't just undergo one feeling at a time. This further convolutes the murky waters we sail upon, clouding our perspective and ability to make good life choices. This chapter explores the vast world of emotions, their impact, and their power over our daily actions and interactions.

EXPLORING THE WORLD OF EMOTIONS

As we watch the sea swirling with emotions, it can be overwhelming to identify precisely what we feel. The vast sea of emotions contains far more than simple feelings, such as happiness, sadness, surprise, or anger. In fact, there are many emotions beyond these basic or primary ones. Let's explore them now.

Primary and Secondary Emotions

In the world of psychology, psychologists have identified what we call primary and secondary emotions. Primary emotions are the fundamental and instinctual emotions considered universal across cultures. This means these are the emotions all humans experience relatively similarly. They are also considered the building blocks for more complex emotions. Primary emotions include happiness, sadness, anger, fear, disgust, and surprise. Primary emotions are often powerful, which makes them relatively easy to identify. They are believed to be instinctual in nature (Evans, 2023).

Secondary emotions are more complex and often arise from combinations of primary emotions. They can vary in intensity and subtlety. They include love, guilt, shame, jealousy, and pride. You can see from these two lists that primary emotions are easier to identify. Secondary emotions are more difficult not only to identify but to work through as we process many of them at the same time. Secondary emotions are the ones that often push people away from us or are used to protect ourselves in some way (Rich, N.D.).

Cultural and Personal Influences that Impact Emotions

Just as individuals from different cultures may have other foods they eat, different languages they speak, and various holidays they celebrate, the way they express emotions might differ. Deep down, the human experience for everyone is shaped by the same emotions you and I experience each day. However, understanding how different cultures shape others' feelings is vital in communicating effectively with diverse individuals. This mainly plays out with facial expressions. For example, some cultures demonstrate different "display rules" (Tsai, N.D.). These might include the appropriateness of making eye contact or biting one's tongue. There are also cultural differences that exist regarding the recognition of emotional facial expressions. The degree to which various cultures focus on the face and other facial expressions varies by geographical location across the globe.

Understanding the cultural and personal influences that impact emotion is critical to understanding our feelings in general. It also prevents us from making assumptions about another's emotional state. Accurately identifying cultural similarities and discrepancies in emotional expression can provide valuable insights into effective communication and the psychological well-being of ourselves and others. Understanding these similarities and differences can help us foster more substantial emotional intelligence in ourselves and help us relate better to others.

EMOTIONAL INTELLIGENCE: THE KEY TO UNDERSTANDING AND MANAGING EMOTIONS

But what is emotional intelligence anyway? It's one thing to recognize our emotions and be able to name them, but learning how to navigate them on stormy seas is another thing! Emotionally intelligent people, however, do just that! Let's start with a working definition of emotional intelligence, or EQ, and expand upon what it looks like in our daily lives.

If we are out at sea, consider the waves we float upon to be our emotions. When emotionally intelligent, we watch our emotions like waves, recognizing them and allowing them to pass by. We don't become too attached to them; we know they will disappear, altering and changing like the ebb and flow of the tide. When emotionally intelligent, we acknowledge and accept them but don't hold on too tight.

understanding, using, and managing emotions effectively (Nemours Teens Health, n.d.). Just like IQ measures intellectual ability, EQ measures emotional intelligence. As IQ predicts test scores, EQ predicts how we will perform in social settings or respond to emotional events.

Emotional intelligence is understanding, using, and managing our emotions effectively.

In other words, whereas a higher IQ is sometimes considered book smart, a higher EQ is considered people smart. EQ is the business of navigating people through a deep understanding of emotions.

But how does EQ develop? How do we learn to navigate the various emotions we experience daily? Let's dig into a few strategies to help!

STRATEGIES FOR MANAGING EMOTIONS

Developing EQ Among the Stormy Waters of Life	

Name the Emotion	• Identify the primary emotion you are experiencing. Primary emotions include:
	  o happy
	  o sad
	  o angry
	  o surprised
	  o disgusted
	  o fearful
	• Secondary emotions are our responses to the primary emotions (whereas primary emotions are typically a response to a situation we have just experienced). If you can, seek to identify your secondary emotions. It could help to use a feeling wheel if you are unfamiliar with secondary emotions, such as the one found here.

Make It a Habit	It can be easy to go all day without getting in touch with our emotions. Once you have practiced labeling them, make sure you schedule various times for emotional check-ins. Some good times to check in with yourself include: • upon waking up • at lunch • after a stressful class or event • before bed
Strive to Understand Others	Empathy occurs when we put ourselves in someone else's shoes. When we strive to understand others, we develop stronger relationships. Empathy also helps us navigate high-stress situations such as conflict.

Self-Regulate	When we begin to understand our emotions, we start to see patterns in the way we respond to certain situations. These responses may be called triggers. Self-regulating means we learn when, where, and how to respond and appropriately express ourselves when under stress.
Choose Your Mood	When we learn how to self-regulate, we begin to decide what type of mood we will allow. People with a high EQ know that moods are not something that just happen to us. We have a choice in the matter, friends!

Developing emotional intelligence is a worldwide cruise, not a one-time sailboating experience. In fact, our EQ might be under construction our entire lives! And it's a good thing it is. Can you imagine a bunch of adults running around kicking and screaming whenever they don't get their way?

Some skills are easier than others to acquire. For example, we've most likely all been naming our primary emotions for years! Secondary emotions may be more complicated. And choosing our moods? We could all use a little assistance there! The good news is, like with everything in life, the more we practice, the easier it becomes. Here are some additional strategies for paying greater attention to your emotions.

- **Journal:** Journaling is a process that allows us the time and space necessary to identify our emotions. Journaling can occur at any time of day and need not be a rigid experience. Some people prefer to do a quick brain dump before bed, while others write to clear the cobwebs from their sleep in the morning. There is no right or wrong way to journal. Even a sentence or two can do the trick!

- **Meditate:** Meditation is another practice that forces us to be present here and now. Often, silence will allow us the quiet necessary to identify emotions we have pushed aside during the busyness of the day. If you are new to meditation, several free apps, such as Calm and Insight Timer, are available to students and provide short guided meditations to get you started.
- **Rate your emotions:** We know emotions come and go, and some sure come on stronger than others! It is helpful to rate your emotions on a scale of 1-5 as they come and go throughout your day. 5 would be intense, and one would be incredibly mild.
- **Connect with a trusted adult or friend**: Learn to share your emotions openly. This will help you form stronger connections with the people closest to you. You will also be modeling vulnerability, which increases trust and communication in relationships.

By practicing these strategies, we can learn to manage our emotions and better connect with others, creating a stronger foundation for relationships. Remember that there is no right or wrong way to improve your EQ. Different strategies are going to work differently for everyone. Meditation might work well for your best friend, but if you don't have a quiet space to practice, it might not be your strategy of choice. The important thing is to find a system that resonates with you so you can practice improving your EQ immediately!

Ask the Captain: Practical Advice for Common Emotional Challenges

Ask the Captain

As we round out the first leg of our journey, it's time to hear from YOU! We wanted your burning questions about the journey toward greater emotional intelligence. We asked, and teens just like you answered the call! Here are your questions and the Captain's advice for navigating various emotional challenges.

How can we ever feel like we're enough in the land of social media? I feel like I constantly compare myself to others and will never be good enough, even though I am already overwhelmed with everything I have.

Ahoy there, young sailor! Dealing with the turbulent waters of social media and the comparison game can be challenging. But fear not, my friend! The Captain is here to lend a hand on this daunting voyage at sea!

First and foremost, remember that social media is like the very sea we sail upon. We might grab a video of a dolphin hurdling the waves or an amazing sunset and post it on our highlight reels. We fail to show the world that we got a little seasick when the waves got a bit too high. In other words, social media does not accurately represent the whole journey. So, don't be so hard on yourself for not measuring up to what you see online. It isn't the whole story, lad!

What is more important during this part of the journey is that you set sail on a course of self-discovery. While you're out there riding the waves, take some time to understand your values, interests, and passions. You might be comparing yourself to someone who, in all honesty, just doesn't tick like you! Knowing who you are and what you stand for is like a sturdy anchor in stormy seas, helping you stay grounded amidst the waves of comparison.

Gather a crew of your most supportive, trustworthy mentors and friends. Surround yourself with people who lift you up and encourage your growth. A strong support system can help you weather the storms of self-doubt and keep your spirits high.

Also, practice gratitude each day. Take a moment to pause and feel the wind in your hair, appreciating your life's little victories and blessings. This keeps you focused on your own inner journey rather than feeling the need to constantly compare it to others'.

Remember, my young sailor, your worth is not determined by likes, comments, or followers. Your worth is determined by the quality of your character and how you treat others in the world. This is your journey - made for you, by you, and nobody else. Hoist your sails high, steer your ship with confidence, and know the real treasure of the sea is you.

How can we deal with authoritarian, toxic relationships when we have no choice?

Ahoy, young matey! Navigating the choppy waters of dealing with authoritarian, toxic folks can be challenging. Over the years, I have had a crew member or two who have exhibited some toxic traits. The good news is, I have plenty of experience in the matter! The Captain is here to steer you through these tricky seas!

When you find yourself in the company of such individuals and have no choice but to interact with them, remember the first rule of the high seas: maintain your calm and composure. Toxic folks often thrive on emotional reactions, so staying composed is your anchor in this situation.

Next, as we steer our ship's course, we must set clear boundaries. It is okay to politely but firmly let people know what behaviors you will and will not tolerate. Hold the ship's wheel tightly and stick to your boundaries. They will protect you from emotional turmoil and pain.

You can also support the rumbles of the seas by getting quiet and practicing active listening. Sometimes authoritarian, toxic folks just need to be heard. By actively listening, you might be able to uncover the root of their discontent and negative energy. You might even find ways to address their problems more effectively in this way!

When all else fails, keep a safe distance, just as you do with dangerous waters when the red flags wave. Limit your interactions to what is absolutely necessary, and avoid engaging in arguments or conflicts. Toxic people can really thrive on dragging others into their drama and misery.

Also, don't forget to rely on your crew. Talk to family, friends, or mentors about the challenges you are experiencing. They know you and may even know the person dragging you down. They can provide valuable advice, encouragement, and a safe harbor when you feel alone at sea.

Always remember, young mariner, this journey is yours and yours alone. You have the power to navigate it in a way that protects your personal integrity and well-being. Stay true to your course and let the toxic waters roll off your back. You're stronger than you think, and you can weather any storm that comes your way.

How can I possibly develop all the social skills I need to be a well-rounded, effective adult?

Ahoy there! Setting your sights on mastering the social skills necessary for adulthood, are ye? Well, you've certainly embarked on quite the adventure. But fear not! The Captain has a few navigational tips to help you chart your course!

First, understand that developing social skills is not a one-time event. It's a journey, not a short one-hour cruise at sea! So, be patient with yourself along the way. Know that each of these skills will develop over time. This isn't a sprint. It's a marathon.

The first tip I will give you is to observe and learn simply. That's really all you gotta do to start! Just like a keen lookout from the watchtower, simply sit back and observe how people react in different situations. Pay attention to their body language, tone of voice, and other unspoken cues that can tell you about a person's feelings or intentions. You can learn a lot from observing how others react in various scenarios.

Next, engage in conversation! Even when you feel a little uncomfortable with the seas, strike up a dialogue with whoever is around. Practice speaking to different people in different settings, and you will naturally start to gain confidence as your speech becomes more assertive and clear. On the ship, you will learn how to talk to brand-new boaters one way and industry professionals in another. Practice makes perfect, sailor!

We also can't forget that part of communicating is actively listening. Just like we listen to the wind and waves at sea to hear what the ocean is telling us, it is imperative that we listen to other people this way, too! Give them your full attention, ask questions, and show genuine interest in what they have to share. This makes everyone on the ship feel valued, regardless of their contribution level or experience.

And speaking of making people feel valued, that sounds an awful lot like empathy to me! Do you see how these social skills all become deeply intertwined? When we listen to understand, we start to see the world from other peoples' perspectives, just as we navigate the sea by stars. Empathy is the compass that guides us in building meaningful connections necessary for our journey. When we seek to understand others' feelings, concerns, and needs, we develop this necessary trait to keep our relationships firmly anchored where we need them to be.

And finally, commit to learning from your mistakes. We are all going to make them! We just have to learn to adjust our course after we get off track. Mistakes are valuable lessons in our journey towards mastering social skills. Learn from them and keep sailing forward.

How do I handle anxiety as a teen?

Ahoy, matey! Anxiety can certainly feel like a storm constantly lurking at sea. Captain Guidance is here to help you navigate these turbulent waters. Here are some tips for navigating anxiety when it threatens to ride in like the waves at high tide.

1. **Know your ship.** Just as a sea captain makes it a point to know every nook and cranny of their vessel, you must know yourself! What triggers your anxiety, and how does it manifest? This self-awareness will serve as your compass.
2. **Crew support.** A wise captain knows that his crew is critical to his success. Reach out to trusted friends, family members, or school staff when you start to feel anxious. Sharing our anxieties helps lighten unnecessary burdens we carry.
3. **Establish a smooth sailing routine.** Just like ships have regularly scheduled maintenance to keep it all intact, we stabilize our moods and ground ourselves in the present when we establish routines. Since anxiety happens when we worry about the future, the present is a great place to be! Consider establishing a regular sleep, exercise, and healthy meal schedule to keep your course on track.
4. **Cabin cleanup.** Aside from regular maintenance, we sometimes need to clean up the cabin to clear the clutter from our heads! Journaling and meditation can both help clear the mental clutter and get us more in tune with our feelings, fears, and hopes.
5. **Chart your course.** Set achievable goals for yourself as a captain chartering a cruise plots his path. Break larger tasks into smaller, more manageable chunks. Achieving them will boost your confidence, and one small victory will start to snowball into several greater ones! When you get off course, simply pause, re-evaluate, and adjust your sails.
6. **Weather the storm.** When anxiety creeps up, which it undoubtedly will, practice coping techniques. When the waves are rising around you, focus on the horizon and take a deep, cleansing breath. Practice box breathing, where you breathe in for four counts, hold for four counts, breathe out for four counts, and hold for one last four count. Repeat this until the storm within starts to calm. Don't forget about positive affirmations, too. Remind yourself of your strengths and abilities. Make a list of everything you love about yourself when that self-doubt creeps in.
7. **Visit the Island of Distraction.** Sometimes, we just need a little escape from the stormy waters of the sea. Engage in a hobby or activity you enjoy - even if it's something little! Walking while listening to your favorite music can be just as engaging as exploring a new island. Pursue your passions, and remember there is more to life than your worries!
8. **Throw up the rescue flares.** If anxiety overwhelms you and you struggle to steer your ship, seek professional help. Counselors, mental health professionals, and trusted adults can all be rescue flares that guide you back to the safety of your ship.

Never forget you are the captain of your ship. While anxiety might occasionally come over you in waves, you can navigate through even the roughest seas with practice and support. Keep your eyes on the horizon. There are always calmer waters ahead.

How can I handle a breakup with emotional intelligence when I am hurting inside?

Ahoy there, young heart! Navigating the rocky seas of a breakup can be a challenging voyage, but fear not! The Captain has been through a few of these before. I am here to support you as we fight against this emotional tempest. Here is how we can handle a breakup with emotional intelligence, even when our hearts are hurting.

First, know that it is necessary to acknowledge your emotions. Just like a seasoned captain faces a turbulent sea with gusto, you must tackle your emotions head-on. Suppressing them or bottling them up will only result in a later explosion of emotions. Feeling sadness, anger, or confusion is okay. Label your emotions and acknowledge that feeling what you feel is right.

Next, know it's okay to share your burden. Just like a ship at sea can't sail without a helping hand, lean on your crew for support! The most trusted individuals in your life are there to help you navigate the emotional waves. Travel to the Island of Distraction together! Go have pizza, catch a movie, or play a sport you all enjoy. Find treasures among the waves as you navigate the healing process.

Also, recognize that this is a time for self-compassion. While it can be tempting to beat yourself up for your perceived mistakes, decide instead to treat yourself with the same love and compassion you would offer a shipmate in distress. Self-compassion is your lifebuoy during tough times. Additionally, practice mindful sailing during this part of your journey. Just as if you were observing the beauty of the sea, focus on the present moment, letting go of past regrets and future worries. Let the sea gently rock you to sleep as you stay present in the here and now.

Reflect and learn. As you begin to chart a new course and set fresh goals and aspirations, remember to review your past voyage. What went well in your relationship? Where were there opportunities for growth? What did you learn, and how did it shape you? This will help you grow in your purpose and excitement for what comes next.

When you struggle, remember that you are your first mate. Limit contact with your ex-partner until the emotional storm subsides. This will help you gain clarity and heal without additional turbulence. Healing takes time. Just as a ship reaches its destination one nautical mile at a time, one foot in front of the other will lead you forward. Be patient with yourself.

Though the seas of heartache can seem endless, with emotional intelligence as your compass, calmer waters will prevail again. Keep your head held high. New horizons await, and your ship will sail stronger than ever before.

Emotional intelligence is just one of the lighthouses we will encounter along this journey to great self-discovery and growth. Let it serve as a beacon in the night when the waters of the sea get rocky. Lean into her light. Listen to her guidance.

She is always beaconing to you in the distance, regardless of the storm.

The North Star's Guiding Light (Key Chapter Takeaways)

- We all experience primary and secondary emotions. Primary emotions provide insight into our initial reactions to an experience or event. Secondary emotions are a reaction to our primary emotions and can push others away if not directly managed.
- Emotional intelligence is the ability to understand, use, and manage our emotions effectively. EQ develops over time.
- Habitually identifying our emotions is an important first step in developing emotional intelligence. Through this process, we learn how to self-regulate and demonstrate empathy for others.
- Journaling, meditating, and other mindfulness activities help us identify our emotions on a regular basis.

2

MAKING CENT$ OF YOUR DOLLAR: A TEEN'S GUIDE TO FINANCIAL LITERACY

I am so glad you rejoined me for our high-seas adventure's next leg! We are quickly approaching another lighthouse, and I am so excited to share her money wisdom with you!

Money wisdom, you ask? That's right! As we dive into financial literacy, this next wave is rolling into our pockets. This chapter's got everything from budgeting basics to wise spending, income, and investing. Just as a captain has to understand their vessel to navigate the waters of life, you too must master money to secure your financial success!

So, let's get started. The first stop on our journey is the Island of Money. Prepare to disembark. There is much to explore!

THE ABCS OF MONEY: INCOME, EXPENSES, AND SAVINGS

Financial literacy is understanding your money and making smart income, expenses, and savings decisions. In the analogy of the ship, your boat is like your financial life.

Financial literacy is understanding your money and making effective income, expenses, and savings decisions.

Your income puts wind in your sails, propelling you forward and allowing you to live your desired life. Income is the money you earn from allowances, part-time work, or other sources.

Expenses are like waves and storms your boat encounters along the way. Expenses include the costs of daily life, such as food, shelter, clothing, and transportation. Intermittent expenses include entertainment and vacations.

Savings are the treasures you stow away in a secret hiding place on your boat. Like a captain gathers supplies for the journey, savings involve setting aside part of your income to prepare for what lies ahead - both the good and the bad!

As you can see, there is much more to collecting a paycheck than just getting paid! We must learn how to use our money effectively to avoid getting stranded at sea. Let's explore some budgeting basics to help you make your money work for the life you want to lead!

BUDGETING BASICS: CREATING YOUR MONEY PLAN

I can already hear your grumblings. Create a money plan. That sounds like work! But budgeting can feel more exciting when you think of it as plotting your course on a map. It's important mainly because if you don't have a plan, it's easy to stray off course, and we don't want anyone stuck out at sea!

A budget is like your financial navigation chart. It helps you determine where your income goes - a concept we call allocation. A budget is a plan to help us allocate our resources wisely. After all, we must cover our expenses while saving for unexpected storms. When we budget, we steer our ship purposefully, ensuring we are constantly on course and financially secure.

But how do we set up a budget? At its most basic level, a budget is just income minus expenses. However, we all know it gets a bit more complicated than that. Since income and expenses vary monthly, a more robust budget can keep us financially stable.

Fortunately, industry experts agree on a few essential overall tips.

How to Create a Financial Roadmap	
Know your income.	Understand how much money you make. • Paychecks and allowances are reliable sources of income. • Do not include bonuses, birthday, or holiday money in your income since they are variable and unstable.
Record your expenses.	Track your expenses for at least an entire week, but preferably for a whole month. • Keep all receipts and track where each dollar goes. • Use a spreadsheet or your bank account as a ledger.
Track spending patterns.	Look at what you *need* to spend versus what you *want* to spend. • Needs might include: school supplies, transportation costs, or phone bills. • Wants could include concert tickets, takeout food, and more. Create a discretionary budget. This is where you divide up your money based on your wants. • If you like to go to the movies each month, you might create a budget for the cost of movie tickets and food. • If you have a particular hobby or you like to buy new apparel each month, create a part of your budget for that.
Subtract the total spent on expenses from your income.	Subtract the amount that you spend on necessities from your total income. • This number tells you what you have left to spend on your wants, or discretionary income, and savings. • Next, subtract from that number what you spent on your

	discretionary income. This gives you the amount you have left for savings. To budget effectively, *you must spend less than you earn!* • If you find that you do not have money left for savings, it's time to go back to your discretionary income and find ways to save.
Create a savings goal.	Being financially literate means having a strong savings plan. • Think about smaller ticket items, such as saving for a new phone or back-to-school clothes. • Larger ticket items also loom on the horizon. What about saving for college, your first apartment, or your very own car?
Decide on how much to save.	There are a variety of ways to save. • **The 50/30/20 Rule.** Using this method, you use 50% of your income on necessities, 30% on wants and discretionary items, and 20% on savings. • **Reverse budgeting.** Reverse budgeting is the idea of putting money into savings first. Next, subtract how much you need for your necessities. What's left over is your discretionary income for your wants. • **Envelope budgeting.** If you're not so great at managing your money, envelope budgeting could be for you! These can be done physically or virtually through various budgeting apps. Designate an envelope for your necessities, savings, and discretionary choices.
Use your budget and stick to it!	A budget only works if you stick to it. Feel free to monitor and adjust your budget as necessary over time.

Even though budgeting may seem complex, the good news is that, like all the skills we are honing during our teenage years, practice makes perfect! You can start budgeting when you receive any income, including allowances received for chores.

Then, get clear on your wants versus your needs. Finally, don't forget to save! Having an emergency fund for a rainy day or when an unexpected fun opportunity lurks on the horizon is always a positive. Having extra money in your pocket for fun always feels good!

THE ABCS OF BANK ACCOUNTS - CHECKING AND SAVINGS

But where do we keep our money? How do we ensure we have the appropriate bank accounts to help us spend wisely and save? The following section will show you how to do just that!

You've started making money. That's great news! But now, what in the world do you do with it? You've progressed past the point of a piggy bank. While keeping some coins around is nice, we're moving way up in the world, friends! The money we will make with increased allowances and first jobs will require something more substantial to keep our money habits on track. That's where your checking account comes in. Listen up! There is important stuff to learn here!

You can consider your bank accounts as safe harbors for your hard-earned money. Your checking account is like a bustling port where you manage your daily expenses. It's easily accessible, like a harbor near your ship's route.

Your savings account functions a bit differently. It's like a hidden cove where your treasures are stored. It's safe, secluded, and perfect for building your financial reserves. Let's learn a little more about how each account functions.

A checking account is a bank account intended to track everyday expenses. Your debit card expenses, online bill payments, and money transfers and withdrawals happen through your checking account. You can open one by visiting a branch of your local bank. You typically need your social security card and a photo ID to open an account. Be sure to check whether the type of checking account you are opening requires any fees. Some bank accounts may require a minimum amount of money in the account each month to avoid fees.

Checking account: A bank deposit account intended to track everyday expenses.

Money enters your checking account through a deposit process. There are three main types of deposits:

- **Cash deposits.** When you deposit cash at a local bank or ATM, the money is available to you in real time without restrictions. This means you can spend, move, or withdraw that money anytime.
- **Check deposits.** When you deposit a check, your bank has to request that money from another bank. Thus, check deposits may take longer to be available for spending than a cash deposit. A check deposit can take one to two business days to show in your bank account. Until the funds are available, the deposit will read on your statement as "pending."

- **Direct deposits.** A direct deposit is one of the quickest ways to receive your paycheck. Using the bank account and routing numbers associated with your account, your employer can directly deposit your paycheck into your checking account.

While checking accounts have much to offer daily, we also need a savings account for that first (or last) 20% of our income. It needs somewhere to go where we won't touch it and it can stay safe. For these instances, we use savings accounts, which are bank accounts where we set aside money for short and long-term goals. These accounts earn interest, which helps our cash grow!

To open a savings account, consider the following:

- Ensure the bank is insured by the FDIC to protect your money.
- Choose a savings account with a high interest rate so you can make as much interest from the bank as possible on your funds.
- Find an account with low to no monthly fees.

You can open a savings account the same way you do a checking account. Visit a local bank branch with your social security card and photo ID, and you will be all set!

Savings account: A bank account to set aside money for short and long-term goals.

Remember that savings accounts typically limit the number of withdrawals you can make. This is typically under six per month, depending on the setup of your account.

SPENDING WISELY: CREDIT CARDS AND MAKING SMART MONEY DECISIONS

Now that we understand budgeting and different account types, we must understand the resources we can use to make daily transactions. The use of cash and checks has declined in recent years, while bank-issued debit and credit cards are more popular ways to spend. Cash apps, such as Venmo and Zelle, have also increased in popularity.

Credit cards are like magical relics on your journey. They can provide you with resources when needed but come with responsibilities. Think of them as powerful tools to help you during emergencies or when making significant purchases. However, just as a captain must use these tools wisely to avoid hidden dangers, you should make intelligent decisions about when and how to use credit cards. Be vigilant and avoid over-spending, just like a captain avoids a rocky shore.

The following chart breaks down some of your most common options for spending your hard-earned dollars:

Money Resource	Pros	Cons
Cash	• Reliable way to pay for years. • Can easily withdraw a set amount for budget-conscious spending.	• No protection if lost or stolen. • Can be difficult to track digitally or with an app when sticking to a budget • Ordering online such as through Amazon, DoorDash, or Uber, prohibits the use of cash as an acceptable payment method.
Debit card	• Linked to money in your checking account. • Can be used relatively universally.	• Potential to overdraw your account, meaning you do not have sufficient funds to make a purchase, although the purchase may go through. Overdrawing an account leads to fees being charged unless you have overdraft protection. • Some debit cards may have monthly deposit and ATM fees.
Credit card	• Allows you to spend the bank's money and pay it back every month. • Offers greater protection against fraud than debit cards. • Can be used to build a good credit history, qualifying	• If you do not pay the card balance off monthly, you will be charged hefty fees and interest rates. • Can allow spending to get out of control if not carefully monitored.

	you for lower interest rates when acquiring a loan, saving on car insurance premiums, and even saving on cell phone contracts	
Money apps (PayPal, Venmo, Zelle, etc.)	• Allow you to move money between friends and acquaintances in an easy manner.	• Transactions are not FDIC insured, meaning your money is not guaranteed to be safe. • Not recommended as a place to store money.

All the money resources mentioned have advantages and disadvantages, and your best choice will be situationally dependent. Consider the pros and cons of using each option for each transaction and determine which resource best meets your current needs. Remember to use credit cards sparingly to avoid racking up unnecessary debt you may not be able to pay off each month.

TAXES AND INSURANCE: UNDERSTANDING THE BASICS

You've heard of taxes and insurance. Unfortunately, income isn't as easy as just collecting a paycheck and moving on. Think of taxes as the lighthouse on the shore that guides your ship safely through the night. Just like a captain must pay attention to the beacon's signals to avoid treacherous rocks, you must also pay attention to taxes!

But what are taxes? Taxes are contributions you make to support the services your city, state, and country provide. This includes education, healthcare, and infrastructure (such as roads and bridges). Taxes are essential to maintaining the safety and prosperity of our financial seas.

Taxes: Contributions made to support the services your city, state, and country provide, such as education, healthcare, and infrastructure.

And insurance? Well, let's imagine that insurance is the lifeboat on our ship. Insurance is there to protect us when those pesky and unexpected storms start to rage. Insurance safeguards our financial well-being just like a captain ensures that lifeboats are ready for emergencies. Insurance provides a safety net in case of accidents, illnesses, or other unexpected events.

Let's break each one of these concepts down now in greater depth.

Taxes

Taxes are mandatory fees that individuals must pay to the government. There are different types of taxes that we pay for different things. Taxes are the primary source of income for the government.

This chart breaks down various types of taxes.

Type of Tax	Short Description	Key Details
Sales Tax	Tax on what you buy.	• Paid by consumers when buying most goods or services. • Provides state and local revenue to cover costs of education, transportation, etc.
Income Tax	Tax on what you earn.	• Paid on the various sources of income you earn. • Can be taken directly from your paycheck. • Major source of income for the federal government, many state governments, and some local governments.
Property Tax	Tax on what you own.	• Source of revenue at the local level. • Provides funding for parks, public safety services, and sometimes additional educational funding.

As you can see, every dollar you pay in taxes will first start as a dollar earned as income. One of the main differences between different types of taxes is when the tax is collected. Here are a few examples:

- If you earn $1,000 on your paycheck in a state with a flat income tax of 10%, $100 in income taxes will be withheld from your paycheck.
- If you purchase a $100 watch from a store with a 5% sales tax, you will pay an additional $5 when you buy the watch.

Tax structures vary between different states and counties. Every dollar you pay in taxes affects the income you can save and spend. It is essential to understand the tax structures where you live so that you can make informed decisions about how to save, spend, where to live, and even how to vote!

Since income taxes can be directly taken from your paycheck, it is crucial to understand what this might look like, primarily when you collect your first paycheck from your first real job! It's important to know what those different numbers mean, as they impact how much take-home income you have.

Here is a brief explanation of a paycheck and accompanying pay stub. We will also explain what you can see on your pay stub and what those things mean!

Paycheck: Payment from an employer to an employee for work done. It can be a physical check or an electronic deposit.

What is a paycheck stub? A pay stub summarizes your earnings and deductions, such as taxes. It contains information on your net and gross income (which we will break down next), state and federal taxes paid, and other deductions, such as healthcare premiums.

Paycheck Stub: A summary of your earnings and deductions.

You should be able to distinguish two types of income - net and gross income. Gross income is what you make before any deductions. Net income is what you receive after taxes and other deductions have been made.

Most employers must provide employees with pay stubs - a record of your wages. A pay stub could be a physical paper or a digital copy of your earnings and deductions. Here is a list of information a pay stub can provide:

- Proof of earnings.
- Necessary information for qualifying for purchasing a car, house, etc.
- Support qualifying for various loans.
- Proof of health benefits.
- Information that eases the process of annually filing taxes.

Here are some codes you might see on your pay stub and what each one means.

Pay Stub Code	Meaning
FED/FIT/FITW	These are federal tax identification codes. The number in this box shows whether you are single or married.
State/SIT/SITW	These are state deduction codes. The number in this box also corresponds to your filing status - single or married.
OASDI/FICA/SS/SOCSEC	These are social security payments. The Social Security program provides retirement and disability to U.S. citizens.
MED	These are Medicare taxes. These taxes fund the Medicare Hospital Insurance program which provides medical benefits for people older than 65 with disabilities.

FSA/HSA	These are health savings.
401(k)	This is a retirement plan. A 401(k) is a separate savings account provided by your employer. It collects a portion of your income and grows with interest over time.
Pay period	This is the date range for when you are being paid.
District/pay location	This is the address where you live. If you move, you must update your address to ensure that you are paying the appropriate taxes.
Leave balance	This is how many days off (sick leave, vacation days, etc.) you have accumulated.
Gross earnings	This is the total number of hours worked and total wages earned during the pay period.
Deductions	This is the total of federal and state taxes deducted from your income to date for the year.
Summary	This summarizes the information on your pay stub overall, including any benefits that are paid by the employer.

A pay stub is like a ship's log. Just like a log record shows essential details about the vessel, a pay stub includes basic information about you and the pay period, serving as the starting point for your financial journey. Your gross income is like a treasure chest, representing the total earnings you have collected on your voyage before any deductions. Your net income is like the provisions you bring on board the ship. This is the total you take home and can utilize to purchase necessities for your journey. Consider your retirement contributions like a lifeboat fund. Just as a good captain sets aside resources for lifeboats, your pay stub includes retirement contributions, helping ensure your safety along your financial voyage.

Whew! That's a lot of information about taxes and paychecks, right, mates? Don't fret. All of this is a learning curve. A pay stub is just a record of your financial journey with crucial details to help you break down where your income goes. Easy, right? Understanding your pay stub carves your way toward a future of excellent financial stability.

But what about insurance? What is it, and how does it come into play? Like retirement, we can consider insurance a part of our financial lifeboat. While our voyage may be fun and adventuresome, it comes with a fair amount of risk and uncertainty. Insurance can be seen as our lifeboat for those moments of "just in case."

Insurance

Insurance is something that protects you financially against the unexpected. An insurance company will pay you if something goes wrong with one of your assets, whether that be your health or your car! Anything that has value can be covered by insurance.

Did you know that some college and professional football players insure their legs to pay them what they might have earned if they suffer a career-ending injury? You can also insure high-dollar items like jewelry, cars, and your house! This protects you against injury, damage, or other loss of the items insured.

We have to assume that life is unpredictable. Storms creep up, such as sudden accidents or illnesses that require additional financial support. Insurance is the lifeboat that comes to our rescue by providing that financial security we need. Insurance coverage shields us from a raging sea. Lose a cell phone? No problem; insurance will help cover the loss! A minor fender bender on the road? Insurance can provide roadside assistance and additional financial support to correct the injury to the car.

How does insurance coverage work?

To have access to insurance, we have to pay a premium. This is usually a monthly fee. When you pay your premium, you allow the insurance company to pay you when an accident, illness, or loss occurs. When one of these situations occurs, you file an insurance claim to alert the insurance company that something has happened.

Here is a breakdown of the types of insurance you will need to consider and what each one provides.

Type of Insurance	Function
Car insurance	This type of insurance covers your car in case of an accident, theft, vandalism, or damage from a natural disaster. • Car insurance may also pay for injuries to another person injured in an accident or for damage to that person's vehicle.
Home insurance	Home insurance covers inside and outside damage to a home, including theft, damage of belongings, and injury to people on the property. • If you do not own the home, you may be required to hold renter's insurance, which covers the same type of unexpected events.

Life insurance	Life insurance supports a person's family in case of a death. • Can support mortgage payments. • Can support college funds. • Is paid out upon death.
Health insurance	Health insurance helps cover doctor's appointments, medications, dental and vision care, therapy, and more. • Some employers provide partial or complete health benefits to their employees. • Sometimes you have to pay a co-pay or premiums for your health insurance.

You can shop around for most types of insurance, so take your time when selecting a plan with premiums that work best for you. Plans vary based on the premiums charged and the types of coverage provided. You can use several sources of online comparison generators to distinguish which plan and company may be best for you.

HANDS-ON FINANCIAL LITERACY: PRACTICAL EXERCISES

This chapter has been packed with valuable information regarding your sail on the sea of financial responsibility. But how do we practice these skills in real life? This final section will bring all this heavy content to life in a fun and engaging way so it all makes sense to you!

The Budgeting Game. This game will provide real-world information about a potential first budget when you get your first job. If you already have one, great! If not, don't worry! We can still make this a fun voyage for you.

- If you are currently employed, access your two most recent pay stubs. We will use this information to create your monthly budget. If you are unemployed, research the pay for a posted job in your area, such as a hostess at a local restaurant or a bagger at your local grocery store.
- Create a budget using your income, expenses, and desired savings. Use one of the methods presented in this chapter to help!
- Discuss your budget with a trusted adult and make any adjustments as your needs and wants change.

Grocery Shopping Challenge. Take a field trip to the local grocery store utilizing a set budget provided by a trusted adult. The challenge is buying your family a week's worth of groceries while staying within the budget.

- Plan your menu before visiting the store. What meals can you prepare that will minimize your spending for the week?
- Price compare. Are there coupons and deals that are better at one store than another? Is it worth it to visit multiple stores to save?

Financial Goal Vision Board. Create a vision board that highlights your financial goals. Consider including current and future aspirations, such as your first car, college, dream home, or perfect vacation.

- Discuss your vision board with a trusted adult and how you plan to save for and achieve various goals.

A list of additional activities and resources will be linked at the end of this book for those looking to take an even deeper dive into financial literacy. The main objective? Have FUN with this new learning! The more you play with budgeting and goal-setting tools now, the more prosperous your financial future will be!

As you set sail on the seas of financial responsibility, remember that understanding the ABCs of money, budgeting wisely, managing bank accounts, and using credit cards responsibly are like the navigational skills a seasoned captain uses to sail the high seas. With these skills, you can confidently steer your financial ship towards a prosperous and secure future.

And now, it's time for everyone's favorite game! Before we wrap up the chapter, let's play Ask the Captain!

Ask the Captain: Practical Advice for Common Financial Literacy Questions

Ask the Captain

Captain! I keep hearing about this thing called a 'credit score.' What is it, and why is everyone talking about it?

Hello there, good matie! I can certainly understand your puzzlement! A credit score can feel like the wind in your sails when it's high and can suck the life out of 'em when it is low. Basically, a credit score shows how reliable you are when borrowing money. Making your payments on time, keeping low debt levels, and being a responsible borrower (such as not opening too many credit cards) can all keep your credit score high. The higher the score, the better the interest rates you can get on loans, such as for a new car or, eventually, a new home.

Ahoy, Captain! I am still experiencing some fog on the seas. Can you help me better understand the difference between a credit and debit card? They look exactly the same to me!

Fret not, young buccaneer! This is a common misunderstanding when we start to really grasp control of our money for the first time. Although debit and credit cards look the same, we can't confuse them for what they are. Paying for something with your debit card is basically like opening up your treasure chest and paying for goods with what you already have. Debit cards deduct money already in your bank account to pay for your worldly loot.

On the other hand, credit cards are used when you borrow money from another shipmate and have to pay him back with interest. In this case, the shipmate is a bank, and the bank charges you to borrow money for your purchase. You have to pay the bank back with some additional money, known as interest. It's always best to make purchases with money you already have if you can help it.

Captain! How do I avoid falling into debt?

Debt can be a treacherous sea monster, my matey! It is best to avoid this monster at all costs using strategies like these:

1. It's helpful to follow a budget to avoid falling into debt.
2. Tally up all your income and expenses. Make a nice, long list! Draw up a map of where your gold is going, and include what you're saving for the future.
3. Make your list of needs versus wants.

Remember that the necessary supplies you keep on your ship are your needs. They're things like food, shelter, and anything else you might need to survive. Your wants are those sparkly trinkets that would be nice to have. They aren't necessary, but they are the icing on the cake! Finally, to steer clear of the debt monster, only spend what you can readily repay. Be mindful of credit card spending to always keep your ship afloat!

Captain, what is an emergency fund, and why is it important?

What a great question, matey! An emergency fund is like a lifeboat for your finances! It's a stash of gold you keep hidden away to deal with unexpected storms and tragedies. Emergency funds keep your boat afloat when the storm comes a-knockin'. It helps you be prepared for whatever the waves toss at you so you don't have to stress during the storm.

So there ye have it, me hearties! That's about all the financial wisdom I have to impart. Follow these lessons and you'll be well on your way to being a savvy sailor on the high financial seas. Fair winds and safe journeys to you all!

The North Star's Guiding Light (Key Chapter Takeaways)

- Income, expenses, and savings are the three primary areas of an effective budget. Planning for and saving about 20% of your income for an emergency fund or future short and long-term goals is recommended.
- Creating and sticking to a budget is one of the keys to effective money management. Consider your income and subtract expenses for an easy formula to create your first budget.
- Checking and savings accounts can be used to manage your money safely and are protected through your local bank. You can open a checking and savings account by taking a photo ID and your social security card to a local bank.
- Using credit cards and other money apps can be effective ways to track your spending. Each money resource has pros and cons, so weigh your decisions carefully when deciding which approach to use.
- Taxes are contributions to support your city, state, and country's services, such as education, healthcare, and infrastructure.
- Insurance protects you from the unexpected by paying various premiums to the insurance company through which you are insured.

3

THE ART OF CONNECTION: BUILDING HEALTHY RELATIONSHIPS

W elcome back! We are excited to have you back for the next part of our voyage - and we are exploring some diverse waters out at sea! Just like the waves of the sea come with a variety of personalities, we will experience a variety of personalities and relationships on our own voyage through life. This chapter will help us explore those relationships and how to make them as healthy as possible!

THE HEART OF THE MATTER: DIFFERENT TYPES OF RELATIONSHIPS

As teens, our relationships tend to shift quite rapidly. Our peer, romantic, and familial relationships, as well as our relationship with ourselves, all evolve. As we strive for more independence, we create new dynamics with our families and focus more on shifting social relationships with our peers. In this section, we will detail each one so that you can better understand how these types of relationships evolve.

Relationship with Self

In our teens, we start to understand ourselves in different ways. We become increasingly independent, more aware of our identity, and experience changes in our self-esteem.

As we strive towards greater independence from our parents, we exercise greater judgment and make more informed decisions for ourselves. We start to solve our own problems through logical reasoning and dependence on our intuition as we gain emotional intelligence and the ability to self-regulate. As we progress through our teen years, we start having thoughts and feelings about our futures and how we would like our lives to progress. We start thinking about college, future careers, and what kind of relationship we want.

As we are gaining independence, we also start to clarify our identities. Identity can be described as our personality or our sense of self. We mature into our bodies, becoming more comfortable with our appearances. We also develop our minds as we learn triggers and how to self-regulate and problem-solve in various circumstances. Sometimes, we don't like certain character traits that have developed, and we work to evolve from them. Other times, we gain self-confidence in who we are as individuals and learn how to leverage our strengths to our advantage.

As we get clear on our own identity, our self-esteem also begins to shift. Self-esteem is basically the way we feel about ourselves.

As we start to hit puberty, our self-esteem naturally seems to drop. Our bodies change, we are exposed to new thoughts, and our perspective of the world begins to shift. We become more thoughtful about who we have been and who we desire to be. When we look at our patterns of thought and behavior, we can become highly critical of ourselves, exposing ourselves to excessive judgment and fault-finding. This can be particularly true in the area of physical appearance. As we grow and mature, however, we become more accepting of who we are and better equipped with the tools necessary to change what requires our attention.

As if that weren't already complicated enough, all these other people are also around! And our relationships with them are shifting, too!

Relationships with Peers

Changing peer dynamics is a typical part of adolescent growth. As we move away in independence from our parents, our attention shifts to our peers and our friends. We feel more understood and accepted by our peers than our family members during this season of our lives.

Teens tend to develop friendships with people with similar interests, social class, and ethnic backgrounds. When we were little, we were typically friends with people in our nearby proximity (neighbors, classmates, sports teammates, etc.), but as we move into adolescence, we tend to nurture relationships with people who share common values, beliefs, and interests. Females specifically tend to develop very close and intimate relationships during this time. Through conversation, they explore their changing identities and sense of self. Males tend to confirm worth through actions rather than personal dialogue and discussion.

Romantic Relationships

Romantic relationships tend to be guided by cultural and societal influences and expectations. We learn these dynamics through observation and practice. Part of physically maturing is learning to control new romantic urges and challenges.

Part of the struggle during adolescence is learning how to self-regulate when hormones shift. Impulsive behavior, shared mutual exploring, and even intercourse are challenges teens will face. Fundamental biological differences also impact how we communicate with people we like or even love. Conflict can be high during the transitions into and out of a romantic relationship during the teenage years.

Familial Relationships

We already know that, during adolescence, becoming increasingly independent from our families is a natural part of maturation. However, during this time, we are also discovering how we feel about our families and their unique dynamics. Suddenly, we start to see our parents or guardians as humans. They don't know everything, after all! We see them in their humanity, witnessing their mistakes and discovering what they may not know. Some elements of rebellion may occur, although they typically de-escalate over time. During this time, it can be natural for relationships with mothers to shift more than those with fathers.

BUILDING BLOCKS: ELEMENTS OF HEALTHY RELATIONSHIPS

Wow! That sure seems like a lot to juggle, right? Not only are we evolving as humans, but now we have peers, romantic partners, and parents to deal with, too? It can seem overwhelming, but fret not! That's why we're here! We have a breakdown of all the elements necessary to build healthy, lasting relationships with those you know and love.

The Centers for Disease Control (2005) gives us a variety of characteristics of both healthy and unhealthy relationships. Let's explore the list together now.

Healthy Relationships	Unhealthy Relationships
Mutual respect	Disrespect
Trust	Distrust
Honesty	Dishonesty
Compromise	Control
Individuality	Dependence
Good communication	Poor communication
Anger control	Hostility and lashing out
Fighting fair	Intimidation or physical violence
Problem-solving	Complicating or neglecting
Understanding	Misunderstanding
Self-confidence	Insecurity and doubt
Healthy sexual relationship	Sexual violence

Let's break down some main elements that can help us build a foundation for a lasting relationship in all the different relationship dynamics in our lives!

- **Respect.** When two people respect one another, they value each other's thoughts, opinions, ideas, and boundaries. You make space for each person's perspective in the relationship.
- **Trust.** In a trusting relationship, two people firmly believe in their partner's reliability, truth, ability, or strength. They have faith in and put trust in each other.
- **Honesty.** When both people are open and truthful with each other, they exude honesty. If there is not honesty in a relationship, trust and respect both suffer.
- **Communication.** Actively listening and talking are part of open lines of communication in a relationship. Strong communication involves listening to understand, not to respond. Effective communication is honest, fair, and kind.
- **Compromise.** When two people agree to give and take in a relationship and master the art of empathy, or putting themselves in someone else's shoes, compromise occurs. Compromise is recognizing different perspectives and finding common ground.
- **Individuality.** When both parties in a relationship respect each other's independence, likes and dislikes, activities, and interests, they honor each other's uniqueness. They recognize each person's unique nature and encourage them to hone their own talents and gifts.
- **Self-Confidence.** When you're self-confident, you know yourself - a primary element of an effective relationship. When you love yourself, you will find that

you are modeling how you want and desire to be
treated by your partner.

We learned about many of these characteristics in our deep dive
into emotional intelligence in Chapter 1. To maintain healthy
connections with those we love, however, we must also learn to
recognize unhealthy elements in a relationship. When these
elements are present, it is time to re-evaluate the relationship
and determine the impact and cost to your life and well-being
during this already tumultuous time of being a teen.

- **Control.** When someone tries to claim power over you
  and your decisions, that is a form of control. Control
  can also be attempting to isolate someone from family
  or friends. Some partners might even try to manipulate
  you into thinking that some of these decisions are
  yours.
- **Dishonesty.** Lying or withholding information are both
  forms of deception. When we are not truthful with our
  partners, we are exhibiting a form of dishonesty.
- **Disrespect.** Disrespect can manifest in several ways.
  Making fun of someone, name-calling, taunting, and
  raising one's voice are all disrespectful. Disrespect can
  also be physical. Harming another person or another
  person's possessions is a form of disrespect.
- **Dependence.** When someone behaves in a way that
  makes you believe their entire identity is tied to you,
  that can be a form of dependence. While phrases such
  as "I can't live without you!" can seem romantic, they
  can also indicate a dependent relationship. When a

partner claims they may hurt or kill themselves because of you, that is a sign of dependence.

- **Physical Violence.** Any form of unwanted touch can be deemed as physical violence. Examples include hitting, slapping, pushing, punching, hair-pulling, and choking. All are forms of abuse.
- **Sexual Violence.** Any pressure to perform sexual acts you are uncomfortable with is a form of sexual violence. If you do not consent - even if you have given it before - it is considered sexual violence and abuse.

It is essential to know that most relationships exist on a spectrum between healthy and abusive, with unhealthy lying in between. There will always be some aspects of our relationships that are healthy and some that are not. Still, it should be considered a red flag when abuse starts to creep into a relationship. While control, for example, may not seem abusive at first, it can lead to physical violence and harm. While blaming may seem relatively harmless after you make up for a fight, it could lead to threatening, more harmful communication down the road.

NAVIGATING CHOPPY WATERS: MANAGING CONFLICT IN RELATIONSHIPS

Ahoy, brave navigators! This has been heavy, right? Remember, though, that every sailor encounters stormy seas from time to time! As we grow and relationships begin to change, conflicts will undoubtedly arise. We will equip you with all the skills necessary to help you navigate the rough waters that sometimes come with the stormy seas of conflict. As skilled sailors use their expertise to overcome high winds and waves, you can harness communication, compromise, and empathy to sail through relationship challenges. Let's start charting a course through these choppy waters together!

Have you heard of conflict resolution? If so, you might already have some of the skills we will discuss in place. If not, fear not, young sailor! We will equip you with all the skills you need to work out some of the most challenging obstacles in your current relationships - no matter who the relationship is with!

Conflict resolution is a style or method to think through and solve complex confrontations, stress, personal problems, and hurt. Even though conflict is a natural part of life and navigating relationships with ourselves, our peers, and our families, we can still equip ourselves with the skills to deal with it more effectively. Conflict resolution reduces the impact of hormonal and emotional changes occurring inside our bodies during our teenage years, keeping important relationships intact. Whereas you might once have flown off the handle when conflict presented itself in your relationships, you will now find that you have the skills to make disagreements more manageable in all aspects of your life. Remember, conflict doesn't have to be negative. We can use our resources to change conflict into good!

Here are some common tips and tricks for navigating unexpected waves in relationships as you ride the sea of change.

First, as unwanted as conflict may be, we must accept that conflict is a reality we all will face. Although it can be easy to want to hide from it, when we accept that conflict is a natural part of life, we can make a choice to resolve it using a variety of different approaches rather than run away from it, which never solves the conflict and often times lets it fester. Wishing circumstances were different does little to change the situation. We have to confront the problem head-on. Here's how:

- **Address the problem and not the person.** It can be easy to want to play the blame game in conflict. "If he/she would only" and "It's his/her fault" are easy scapegoats; however, they only project the problem onto another individual and create additional relationship struggles. Avoiding making it personal can help us see the situation more objectively.
- **Practice active listening.** Suppose we know we have a problem and decide not to project that problem onto another person. In that case, we can be more respectful of the other individual(s) involved. Listen to the other party or parties intending to understand, not necessarily to be understood. Get quiet and seek to understand the problem from the other person's perspective. Put yourself in their shoes. This is a form of practicing empathy, making others feel valued and respected while maintaining their dignity.
- **Express yourself calmly but assertively.** Just because you listen to another person's perspective does not mean that your own thoughts and opinions don't have merit. What matters is the way you choose to express those thoughts and opinions. State your perspective clearly, stating facts and using the "I statement" to

express your feelings. Speak for yourself in the situation and not for others.

- **Honor the art of compromise.** In conflict, it can be tempting to want to "win." However, the desired end result of conflict should not be someone winning and the other person losing. It should be to find common ground by collaborating and working together as a team. What is a resolution that would honor both parties? How can you meet in the middle when you start on opposite sides?
- **Only speak about the present.** Although you may have had conflict with this person before, resolve to stick to the present situation and not drag in events from the past. Avoid over-generalizing, such as saying "you always" or "you never." Resolve to stick to the present situation and don't sling mud about past mistakes.
- **Apologize.** When you are wrong, be humble and admit it! It's okay to mess up every now and then. When we can speak honestly about our mistakes, it helps others recognize what it means to be vulnerable. They might also open up and apologize for their role in the conflict!
- **Practice the art of forgiveness.** Regardless of the outcome, resolve to practice grace and forgiveness. No one is perfect - not even us! Let go of what cannot be resolved and wish the other party well if a resolution cannot be found. Learn from the experience and vow to move forward differently based on your role in the conflict.

There isn't always a proper way to handle conflict. Each situation is unique, and different approaches to conflict resolution may be necessary to resolve different conflicts effectively. In general, however, regardless of the conflict, the following steps can always be taken to improve the situation:

1. Practice active listening.
2. Seek to understand.
3. Accept what cannot be changed.
4. Strive to communicate effectively.
5. Attempt to resolve the issue.
6. Say sorry when necessary.
7. Forgive.

It is also helpful to note that we can minimize opportunities for conflict by working to reduce our personal stress. When we are under stress, we become more easily escalated. This leaves opportunities for conflict to creep up unexpectedly in our lives. Managing our stress through daily mindfulness activities, such as journaling and meditation, can help reduce the tension that leads to unwanted conflict.

We can also avoid conflict by simply practicing and improving our emotional intelligence! Hey, that sounds familiar, right, sailor? When we improve our communication skills, speaking openly, honestly, and transparently with people who hurt us, we can break down barriers that lead to hurtful assumptions and increase the chances of conflict resolution. We can also practice empathy for others by putting ourselves in their shoes and seeking to understand the world from their perspective.

This levels the playing field and makes others feel valued and respected in their own unique humanity.

Although several circumstances might increase conflict in our lives as teens, such as hormonal fluctuations and changing relationship dynamics, we can still practice effective conflict resolution skills that can help keep our most valued relationships intact. Remember, there is always a calm after the storm. Practicing emotional intelligence and effective conflict resolution can help us increase the likelihood of calm seas quicker than hiding from conflict or addressing problems out of anger and frustration.

THE SOCIAL CODE: UNDERSTANDING SOCIAL ETIQUETTE

As we wrap up this dialogue on building healthy relationships, it is time to discuss how our everyday actions and behaviors can help us connect more effectively with the people we know and love. It's time to set our course on civility and courtesy, shipmates!

Just like ships follow navigational coordinates, in relationships, social codes and etiquette guide our interactions with others. These are the rules of human connection, and they make sailing on the vast sea of adolescence easier for us all! Let's dive into a deeper understanding of this social code and how we can leverage etiquette for more effective relationships in all areas of our lives.

Just because we learn manners as kids doesn't mean we are always good at practicing them, am I right, brave sailors? Sometimes, we all need a refresher on how to behave in ways that honor both ourselves and others. As sailors follow specific rules when sailing the open seas, we must also adhere to certain social norms to smooth our interpersonal interactions. Here are some tips and tricks to refresh your memory and help you keep your coveted relationships on board your ship!

- **Apologize when you are wrong.** Imagine a ship at sea. It has accidentally veered off course due to a navigational error. To correct its course, sailors must acknowledge the mistake, apologize to the rest of the crew, and get back on course. Similarly, when we make errors in our relationships, such as hurting someone else's feelings, we must also apologize to correct the course of the relationships. It keeps our social journey on track!
- **Get input from others before making important decisions.** Just like sailors ask permission from their captains before they make certain decisions on board their ships, we should also ask permission before we make important decisions that impact those we know and love. For example, we should never share someone else's personal information without their consent or make decisions for someone they may not want. This ensures smoother sailing on the social waters of our lives.

- **Communicate kindly and with respect.** Consider being on a boat ride with a good friend where you are sitting face to face. It might be easy to divert your attention to the sunset on the horizon or another boat passing by. Sailors must avoid distractions while navigating their ships, however; we should maintain good eye contact with our friends and avoid other unnecessary distractions, such as looking at our phones, when others speak. Good eye contact, nodding, and other active listening skills are necessary to communicate effectively and make the other individual feel valued and respected.

- **Respect other people's personal space.** Boundaries are necessary on the high seas! Respecting buoys and other navigational hazards is essential to keep ships from sailing into shallow waters and rocks. Similarly, respecting personal boundaries is necessary to avoid physically and emotionally hurting others. Please do not take things from others without permission, and always ask permission before touching someone else. Respect boundaries to avoid unnecessary misunderstandings and potential conflict.

- **Mind your manners.** Something as simple as saying "please" and "thank you" can go a long way on the high seas! Additionally, when we need to interrupt or get by someone, saying "excuse me" is also helpful. Consider politeness the anchor that holds your ship steady along its course! When you are out at sea with a crew, sailors express gratitude for other shipmates who help them along the journey. We should express this same attitude

of appreciation for the people we interact with daily.
Being polite helps us navigate social situations with
respect and grace.

- **Talk when it's your turn.** On a ship, the crew must
work together and listen to each other to avoid
potential catastrophes that could occur on stormy seas.
In our relationships, everyone should also have the
opportunity to speak. Waiting our turn to speak and
avoiding interrupting others maintains order on a busy
ship deck.

- **Practice polite introductions.** Have you ever watched
a sailor wave at another sailor at sea? When boats pass
by, nearby vessels practice polite introductions to each
other to ensure everyone feels safe and welcome on the
high seas. When you meet someone, shake hands and
look the person in the eyes, repeating their name and
saying "nice to meet you" if appropriate. Establishing a
friendly connection will leave a positive impression.
You never know whose good grace you may need on
the waters of stormy future seas.

- **Practice good hygiene and personal care.** When out at
sea, sailors often take precautions to prevent illness.
They keep themselves clean, wash their hands regularly,
and cough/sneeze into their elbows to avoid the spread
of germs. Like good sailors, we should also practice
good hygiene and personal care to keep ourselves and
others safe on our ships!

There are, of course, plenty of other social etiquette rules we could discuss. Appropriate language use, proper table manners, and even the art of writing thank-you notes should be preserved in this discussion. And, as always, follow the golden rule. Treat others the way you want to be treated and act around others as you would like them to act around you. If you do this, the rest will usually take care of itself.

In the vast social sea of life, adhering to appropriate etiquette rules is like navigating a ship through calm waters. It helps us maintain harmony in our relationships, demonstrating respect and concern for others, not just ourselves.

And now, it's everyone's favorite part of the voyage! It's Ask the Captain time!

Ask the Captain: Your Relationship Questions Revealed

Ask the Captain

Hey Captain! My partner and I can't seem to stop arguing over every little thing. How can we handle arguments more effectively?

Unfortunately, every ship has its share of storms, me laddie. When conflict brews, as it inevitably will, remember to remain calm first. Take a few deep breaths to steady your heart rate and calm your physiological or bodily reactions to the stress. Then, approach the situation respectfully, even if you disagree with your partner. Actively listen and seek to understand, not to be understood. This means quietly taking in what your partner tells you, repeating what they said, and seeking clarification if you have questions. Then, voice your perspective respectfully. Seek to reach common ground where you both compromise - the give-and-take process. Your goal is to seek a resolution that leaves both of your sails intact.

If you cannot stop arguing regularly, it could also be time to re-evaluate the relationship. Get in touch with your core values and beliefs and determine if you and your partner's goals are aligned.

Captain, everyone says to have healthy boundaries in a relationship, but what does that mean?

Boundaries in a relationship are like borders on a treasure map, young buccaneer! Boundaries define what you're comfortable with and what you're not. When you set them with your partner, you ensure smoother seas ahead.

Boundaries could be placing parameters on how long you will talk or text at night or how much time you will spend together outside of school. You might have boundaries about what you can discuss about your personal relationship or limitations regarding the physical aspects of your relationship. The important thing about boundaries is to communicate them clearly so that you and your partner are on the same page and no one unintentionally rocks the boat!

Yo-ho-ho, Captain! How do I know if I'm in love?

Ahoy, good matie! This is the trickiest question of them all! Love is a grand adventure, me hearties, much like sailing a new ship for the first time. Love is that feeling that fills your heart with joy and happiness when you spend time with or think about the other person. Usually, love stems from trust, admiration, and respect. The first signs of love could be jitters in your tummy or a quickened heartbeat when that special someone is around. That warm and fuzzy feeling? That could be love! Remember, lust is more of a physical attraction, whereas love tends to be based on feelings that stem from knowing another person in an emotionally intimate way.

Ahoy, Captain! What do I do if my partner cheats on me?

These are stormy seas indeed, buccaneer! What to do in this situation depends on you and your personal boundaries, values, and beliefs. Sometimes, in a relationship, people decide to forgive each other for the wrong that was done. They spend time rebuilding trust through open communication and transparency about their feelings and needs. Other times, couples decide that once that violation of trust happens, there is no way to move forward. They move on to clearer skies. The choice is yours based on what you determine is best for you, your values, and your beliefs.

I am ready for my relationship to end, but my partner is not. What should I do?
Sometimes, matey, even the sturdiest ship must be retired if aspects are beyond repair. It is best to be open and honest about your feelings in these situations and respectfully part ways. Remember that charting a new course may be challenging for both of you, especially the one who wants the relationship to continue. Be respectful of your difference of opinions and give each other the space necessary to grieve the relationship and move on.

Captain! I am in a great relationship, but I am losing myself. How can I maintain my identity and be in a relationship simultaneously?
Aye, mate! You are absolutely right! You must be true to yourself, whether in a relationship or not. Even when you share a vessel with someone else, your values and beliefs are still essential to maintain. Maintain your hobbies and interests, and continue to spend time with crewmates outside of your relationship. Balance is vital in any relationship, and healthy boundaries will keep your personal identity intact.

Ahoy, Captain! I suspect some aspects of my relationship might be unhealthy. How do I know?
Beware, me hearties! Signs of an unhealthy vessel are vast! Signs of trouble on the high seas could be control, jealousy, disrespect, and physical or emotional harm. If you are experiencing any of these signs, you should step back and re-evaluate your current relationship. If you spot dark clouds on the horizon, it might be time to jump ship.

Aye, Captain! How can I communicate more effectively with my partner?
Effective communication is like a good compass on a ship - it keeps the vessel on course! Listen with an open heart, speak honestly, and be willing to compromise - just like the ebb and flow of the tides!

Remember, me hearties, a healthy relationship is like sailing calm waters under a blue, clear sky. It brings joy and fulfillment to our hearts! But if you ever find yourself in troubled waters, seek guidance from trusted resources and keep your compass set on respect for yourself and for others. Fair winds and smooth seas to you and every relationship you are in!

The North Star's Guiding Light (Key Chapter Takeaways)

- Adolescence is a period of self-discovery, where individuals become more independent and gain a deeper understanding of their identity and self-esteem.
- Adolescents experience changing peer and familial dynamics as they shift their focus from their parents to their peers. They often feel more understood and accepted by their friends during this phase.
- Healthy relationships are built on mutual respect, trust, honesty, good communication, compromise, and self-confidence.
- Conflict resolution is a valuable skill in maintaining relationships. It involves addressing problems objectively, actively listening, calmly expressing thoughts, compromising, and seeking common ground.
- Managing stress and improving emotional intelligence can reduce the chances of conflict arising.
- Practicing politeness, apologizing when wrong, asking permission, communicating kindly, respecting personal space, and minding manners all contribute to effective social interactions.

4

THE ART OF EXPRESSING YOURSELF

Effective communication is like the rudder that steers our ship through calm and stormy waters in the vast ocean of life. It isn't just the words we use that matter but also how we craft them, listen, and decode the silent signals surrounding every interaction. As we set sail on this voyage in Chapter 4, we will navigate through the essential aspects of communication together. Let's get this ship out to sea!

WORDS MATTER: CRAFTING CLEAR AND EFFECTIVE VERBAL COMMUNICATION

We all know that on the high seas, it isn't just what you say but how you say it that's important. Yet, clear and effective communication doesn't always come naturally when we're out there on rocky waters. We all have different communication styles, and recognizing them can lead to more effective communication as we navigate life's ebbing and flowing tides.

There are four primary communication styles. Passive communication occurs when we are afraid to make someone angry by expressing ourselves or are hiding our feelings to avoid conflict. If you say, "I don't care," or "It doesn't matter," when it actually does, you may be engaging in passive communication.

Aggressive communication is when you say what's on your mind without regard for the other person's feelings. You put your needs in front of the other person's. You may be an aggressive communicator if you yell or swear to get your point across.

A passive-aggressive communicator is - you guessed it - a combination of both of the previous styles. A passive-aggressive communicator utilizes sarcasm or the silent treatment to prove their point.

The assertive communication style is the one we all aspire to achieve. Assertive communicators are open and honest, respectfully asking for what they need. They also listen attentively and consider the other person's perspective with respect.

To be more assertive in your communication, try this:

- **Be direct and clear.** Avoid beating around the bush or using complicated language that can cause your point to be missed. If you need something, ask for it directly and clearly. Do you need help on a big school project? Ask for it! Do you need support from a trusted adult to navigate a sticky situation with a peer? Give the details necessary for the adult to understand. Being direct and clear can help you achieve the desired outcome from your communication.

- **Watch your tone.** How you speak can often carry even more weight than your words! For example, saying "thank you" in a sincere, grateful tone sounds much different than saying the exact same words dismissively or sarcastically.
- **Use "I" statements.** Express your thoughts and opinions from your perspective instead of speaking for others. This also helps us avoid placing blame. For example, instead of saying, "You never listen when I talk," try saying, "I feel ignored and unimportant when I talk and you are scrolling through your phone."

Striving to be more assertive communicators can help us immensely when communicating with diverse shipmates on the seas of life. Being effective communicators isn't just about what we say and how we say it, though. Effective communicators also practice active listening, which is where we're journeying to next!

LISTENING TO UNDERSTAND: THE POWER OF ACTIVE LISTENING

Navigating the seas of communication is a collaborative endeavor. It takes two to tango, right, sailors? To be effective communicators, we must also master the art of active listening. When we fully engage with the speaker, we let them know they are not on a solo voyage adrift in the vast sea of silence.

What does active listening look like? Non-verbal cues, like nodding your head or maintaining eye contact, can be great ways to demonstrate you are tracking with the speaker and internalizing what is being said. Verbal affirmations, such as "uh-huh" or "I get that," demonstrate attentive listening.

This chart shows several techniques to help you practice active listening more effectively.

Technique	Purpose	How-To	Example
Paraphrasing	• Shows interest. • Encourages the speaker to continue.	Restate the information you just heard in your own words.	"So, it sounds like you showed up for rehearsal on time."
Stating emotions	• Shows understanding. • Helps speaker evaluate their own feelings.	Reflect the speaker's feelings in your own words.	"And that made you really frustrated and upset."
Asking questions	• Gathers more information.	Ask questions.	"After you expressed your frustration, how did Amy react?"
Summarizing	• Synthesizes pieces of the conversation to create a holistic overview and draw conclusions. • Establishes how to move the dialogue forward.	Restate major ideas, thoughts, and feelings that were expressed.	"It sounds like you had a difficult start to practice, arriving late and already feeling flustered. When you continued to bat poorly, it sounds like that only made the situation worse. When your coach yelled at you, that seemed to be the final straw."

Clarifying	• Clarifies what was stated. • Helps the person see the situation from a unique perspective.	Ask questions to clarify vague or ambiguous statements.	"You said you overreacted to the situation. Can you describe what that means?"
Encouraging	• Expresses interest and care. • Promotes additional dialogue and sharing.	Express empathy and offer ideas and suggestions as appropriate.	"I know that must have been difficult for you. Go on. What happened after that?"

When practicing active listening, there are a few things to avoid to enhance the power of your connection and communication.

- **Self-monitor for judgment.** Remember, the purpose of actively listening is to provide a safe space for the other party to share freely. This can only happen if we stop criticizing, labeling, or diagnosing the other party.
- **Avoid taking on the role of the 'fixer.'** Although we may mean well, sometimes we like to solve others' problems because we are uncomfortable with their discomfort or pain. We want to fix it all! And while that's great in some circumstances, it can create a disruptive power dynamic. By offering to fix someone else's problem, we disempower them to create their own solutions and risk leaving them feeling less than and unheard.
- **Leave open space for sharing.** It can be tempting to dive into the dialogue with questions and reassurance when we feel the other party is in distress. Seek to keep

conversations open-ended and flowing, even when you want to jump in and help. Your role is to support by listening, not by comforting.

Listening to understand is an art. Although it involves authentic listening and refraining from oversharing and attempting to 'fix' a problem with the other individual, there is also more to active listening than silence and a few words. Now, let's explore what we say when we say nothing!

SILENT SIGNALS: UNDERSTANDING NON-VERBAL COMMUNICATION

Non-verbal communication, including facial expressions, body language, and gestures, can all express what we think and feel beneath the surface. They happen without a word, but they sure do convey a lot! Let's break down these silent signals so they become silent and empowering instead of silent but deadly to our dialogues with those we love.

Facial Expressions

When you look in the mirror, what's reflected back to you? If you are happy and smiling, the mirror literally mirrors how you look and feel! Feeling sad or grumpy? Your mirror will reflect that, too!

Mirroring is no different in critical conversations with others. When we mirror a person we are conversing with, we mimic their emotions and body language. We naturally observe the other party's expressions and gestures, then adopt similar ones to state, "I am with you, and I understand," without using words.

Think about the last time you had an important conversation with someone. If you were discussing a recent breakup with your partner, for example, you probably didn't have a massive smile on your face unless the relationship was pretty bad! If you were crying, however, and your friend was smiling and laughing, you would probably feel shut down and be less willing to continue to share.

The overall gist? Show compassion and empathy by mimicking the other individual's behavior in the conversation. This creates an open dialogue free of judgment that is necessary for effective communication to occur.

Body Language

The body language we utilize in difficult dialogues is also a strong indicator of active listening and can promote effective communication. How we use our heads and bodies can significantly impact the level of communication achieved, especially during difficult dialogues.

First, use your head to nod throughout the conversation. Nodding in a cluster of three at regular intervals throughout the discussion promotes continued dialogue, encouraging the speaker to continue talking. Head tilting is also a universal sign of listening, indicating that you are curious, interested, and engaged in what the other person is saying.

We also reveal much about our listening by opening or closing our body language during dialogue. Closed postures are when the arms and legs are crossed or folders, and the torso or legs are turned away from the person speaking. An open body posture is much more receptive. Arms and legs are uncrossed, feet are flat on the floor, and palms are typically open, signaling the way for an inviting dialogue.

It is also important to remember to lean in. Leaning backward can be a sign of negativity or disapproval, but leaning in is a way to invite further dialogue. When two people like each other, they often lean into the conversation.

Finally, remember to use gestures wisely. When we use overly dramatic gestures, it can be off-putting to the other party. Smaller, natural gestures are better ways to emphasize your point.

Other Important Reminders

Here are a few other things to remember when engaging in effective dialogue. First, you cannot actively listen and simultaneously engage in other tasks. Avoid checking your phone during conversation and make eye contact with the person speaking.

Further, if there are any physical barriers between you and the other person, move them. Even holding a drink directly in front of you can impact the effectiveness of communication between you and the other individual. Some studies have even found that the higher you hold a cup, the more insecure about the conversation you are. Hold your drinks lower towards your chest and to the side of you and the person you are communicating with.

Finally, don't forget to smile. Smiles invite warm and open communication. Smiling also influences the way others respond to you. It can positively trigger their emotional state.

NAVIGATING DIGITAL COMMUNICATION: SOCIAL MEDIA, TEXTING, AND MORE

In today's fast-paced world, communication doesn't only happen in person. In fact, most of our communication occurs digitally through social media, texting, emails, and more. Thus, navigating digital communication requires its own unique set of skills and etiquette.

Although digital communication is an everyday occurrence, it is also relatively complex. When communicating digitally, we lose some of the non-verbal cues that can impact the effectiveness of a conversation. For example, something that comes across jokingly in person could be misconstrued as rude and inappropriate in the virtual setting. Thus, it is essential to consider our word choice carefully in the digital environment since we don't have non-verbal cues to support our intent.

Basic Online Communication Rules

It is essential to consider the type of communication you are crafting to communicate effectively online. For example, while slang and acronyms, such as WYD or LOL, are appropriate in a text communication with a friend, they would not be appropriate in an email to a teacher. Follow grammar and punctuation rules when communicating in a formal online setting.

Also, proofread your work before you send it! Nothing is worse than a misspelled word or poor grammar when trying to create a professional impression. This can be particularly important when using your phone to communicate, as sometimes autocorrect can make a word quite offensive!

Finally, remember not to type in "ALL CAPS." This is considered yelling online.

Considering Social Media

Posting on social media is one of the most important things to consider when planning for effective communication in the digital world. Social media caters to a broad audience, and sometimes even private posts reach more than the intended viewers. It is not uncommon for students to lose scholarships, be denied college admission, or lose job opportunities based on their behavior online.

Remember that if you post something on the internet, it is never completely private, and digital content never really goes away. Even deleted accounts and posts can be screenshot and archived. If you wouldn't want your grandma to know you said it, you might not want to say it!

Also, consider the type of communication necessary to achieve the desired outcome of the conversation. If you have to write more than a few paragraphs, it is better to pick up the phone and ask the other party if they can chat. Texting and social media can cause information to be misconstrued and may lead to increased and unnecessary drama. A give-and-take dialogue can be more effective, especially when conversations are emotional and stressed.

Finally, remember to respect other people's privacy online. Don't share personal information or posts without the express permission of others. It is good practice not to overshare about others what you would not want to share about yourself.

CONFLICT RESOLUTION: COMMUNICATING THROUGH DISAGREEMENTS

Finally, sailors, we can't always count on calm, quiet seas. Conflicts are a natural part of communicating with others, and while challenging, with the right communication skills, we can navigate them effectively and even strengthen our relationships in the process.

First, during conflict, it is crucial to stay calm. It might not be the appropriate time to communicate if you are overly heightened, angry, and frustrated. When you are ready to talk, remain even and respectful. Communicate your feelings without inserting insults or making personal attacks.

In conflict, it is also important to listen more than you speak. Even if you disagree with the other person's perspective, actively listening will help you understand their point of view and can help you seek common ground.

Finally, use your problem-solving skills! Once everyone has had the opportunity to express their feelings, work together to find a potential resolution. This could be a compromise, or sometimes it might mean simply agreeing to disagree.

And now, it's time for everyone's favorite game. Let's Ask the Captain!

Ask the Captain: Your Communication Questions Revealed!

Ask the Captain

Avast, Captain! What should I do if I get into a disagreement with a friend?

Disagreements are like stormy seas, me matey! They are just unavoidable at times. To navigate them well, remember first to stay calm and be respectful. Then, be willing to listen to the other person's point of view. Together, you will find yer way to brighter skies and compromise.

Captain, what is the key to communicating better with others?

Aye, me laddie! The key to communication is like charting a new course on a map. We have to start with clarity to be understood. Use clear and direct language so that your message sails straight and true to its destination.

Captain, how do I handle rumors and gossip?

Rumors and gossip sure are tough, me matey! Rumors remind me of barnacles on the side of the ship. It's better to scrape them off and avoid spreading them around! If you hear them, remember not to jump to conclusions. If you hear something about someone that concerns you, go to that person directly and handle the situation privately between the two of you.

Avast, Cap'n! What is the secret to keeping a conversation going smoothly when there is a lot at stake?

It's always good to have strategies for keeping a conversation going smoothly! To keep a dialogue flowing like a gentle current, ask open-ended questions. These are questions that can't be answered with a simple "yes" or "no." Open-ended questions encourage deeper, richer dialogue and allow each party to express themselves.

Learning and practicing effective communication skills allows you to express yourself clearly, understand others better, and confidently navigate various social situations. From your relationships with friends and family to future job interviews and workplace interactions, these skills will serve you well throughout your life.

The North Star's Guiding Light (Key Chapter Takeaways)

- Effective communication isn't just about what you say but how you say it.
- Strive to be an assertive communicator by being clear and direct, watching your tone, and using "I" statements.
- Active listening involves engaging with the speaker through non-verbal cues and verbal affirmations.
- Non-verbal cues, including facial expressions, body language, and gestures, convey thoughts and feelings.
- Mirroring another person's emotions and body language can foster empathy and connection.
- Digital communication requires unique skills and etiquette. Be mindful of word choice, and remember that digital content is rarely completely private.
- In conflict, stay calm and respectful, avoiding insults and personal attacks.

5

CHARTING YOUR OWN PATH: THE ART OF INFORMED DECISION-MAKING

As we continue to sail forward on this voyage of self-discovery and growth, we find ourselves navigating the waters of decision-making. Every choice we make is like a new course correction on our journey. Understanding how to make informed decisions is the compass that guides us through the vast sea of possibilities.

THE POWER OF INFORMED DECISIONS

Understanding the value of making informed decisions can empower you to take control of your life and future. For example, even though they may be challenging, taking advanced math classes in high school opens more opportunities for college majors in STEM (science, technology, engineering, and mathematics). When you decide to learn how to drive, you open up more opportunities to find a job and volunteer in your community. You gain mobility and independence. On the flip side, if we don't learn to make informed decisions, we can easily steer our ships off course. If we decide to get into a car with someone who has been drinking, for example, we could easily find ourselves not just in legal trouble but facing the consequences of injury or even death.

Making informed decisions goes beyond a gut feeling or peer pressure. Decision-making is a thought-out process that considers our choices' potential outcomes and consequences. Once we have all the information we need, we can weigh our decisions' benefits and risks and determine which choice is right for us. After considering everything involved with our options, we can look at our goals and what we want to accomplish and make the right choice based on the pathway of our lives.

Here are other reasons why informed decision-making is so important:

- **Informed decisions improve self-confidence.** When we make informed decisions, we feel more confident that we have made the right choice for ourselves and avoid second-guessing our actions.
- **Informed decision-making increases our knowledge and our options.** When we research and consider our options before making a choice, we naturally become more knowledgeable about our decisions. We often uncover other opportunities and solutions that increase our capacity to make good choices.

- **Informed decisions give us more control.** We have greater power over our decisions after considering all the variables and options.

UNPACKING THE DECISION-MAKING PROCESS

Effective decision-making involves identifying options, evaluating them, and choosing the best choice for you. Here are some steps you can follow.

Determine the decision that needs to be made. Let's say you want to consider joining a club. You first need to identify what clubs are available to join. You might have three options that work for you. Drama club, chess club, or robotics meet on the dates and times you have available each week. You must decide which club you want to join.

Gather information. There are questions you can ask that will facilitate the decision-making process.

a) How will this decision or change affect me?
b) What does my gut tell me about this decision?
c) How does this decision impact my short and long-term goals?
d) What options do I have?
e) What are the adverse effects of each option available?
f) Am I in the right mindset to make this decision? Is now the appropriate time?

Research. Depending on the type of decision you are making, you may need to conduct some research to gather additional information. For example, comparing your three club options with your future college goals might require digging deeper into majors, college credit, and eventual careers.

Consider all possible outcomes. Compare the positive and negative components of each available option . Create a pro and con list for each decision and use the lists to help you identify the best option. For example, a pro of joining the drama club may be that you like the teacher who facilitates it, but a con may be that you don't enjoy speaking in public.

Make a decision. After comparing all possible options, determine which one you will choose. You may like math more than public speaking, so you decide to join the robotics club, and you have some friends who are already members.

Evaluate the outcome of your choice. After some time has passed, evaluate your decision. Did it work out as you expected? Is there anything you would change? What will you do differently next time?

Informed decision-making, especially when choices are high-stakes, can be an overwhelming process. Many emotions can quickly escalate throughout the process, depending on the stress of the decision. Here are a few additional tips that can further support you during these high-stakes decisions.

- **Take an appropriate amount of time to choose.** Although you have to be careful not to let too much time pass on some decisions, you also need to allow yourself time to go through the decision-making process. Determine the time necessary to decide and any pending deadlines for your choice. Then, allocate your time appropriately.

- **Share your ideas with others.** Bouncing ideas off family, friends, and other trusted adult advocates is always helpful. If you are deciding on a future college, talk to a current student or recent alum. If you are trying to determine what club to join, ask current members what they like most about their experience.
- **Do not make decisions when you are feeling emotional.** Respect your humanity. Sleep on it if necessary. Circumstances frequently look and feel differently in the morning.

Always keep in mind that every decision we make has consequences. Just like the tides ebb and flow, your choices will have a lasting impact on your journey. Consider the long-term implications of your decisions carefully. Your future will thank you!

OVERCOMING DECISION-MAKING PRESSURE

The pressure of decision-making can be as overwhelming as a sudden storm at sea. Sometimes, this pressure causes stress and anxiety, disrupting our lives. We can, however, use various tools to help us manage pressure as we navigate through the sea of decisiveness.

Let's consider a college scenario. You have selected the university you believe offers the most opportunity for academic and personal growth, and now you are pressured to choose your major. You have a lot of interests, and the path forward isn't readily discernible. You feel like if you don't make the right choice early in your college experience, you will waste time and money due to the unknown.

Remember that although pressure feels high when these high-stakes decisions appear, few decisions in life are irreversible. Many successful sailors change course and even their ships entirely throughout their lives. Knowing there is always the ability to change can take unnecessary pressure off the decision-making process.

To manage decision-making pressure, prioritize your choices and break them down into manageable parts. For example, rather than trying to plan your entire university career, look first at fulfilling your non-major-specific requirements. You will probably need some combination of math, English, and humanities or science courses, along with other potential electives. Use these electives to explore areas of interest you may need to learn more about. You might also attend workshops, research internships, or take short online courses to gain experience and additional knowledge.

Remember that we will all make mistakes along our journey, even after chunking our decisions into more manageable parts. We might make an informed decision about our college major after taking a great Introduction to Psychology class. We feel excited about the realm we are learning about and decide this is our major. However, once we get some lab experience, we might find that the spark has dulled, and we definitely are not interested in working in a lab. It's okay to change course. Most decisions are not permanent. It's okay to not always get it right.

REAL-LIFE SCENARIOS TO PRACTICE DECISION-MAKING SKILLS

As you sail through the waters of life, you will encounter plenty of decision-making opportunities where you can practice the content of this chapter. They are probably all around you right now! Some decisions may be as simple as choosing whether to attend an event or study for a crucial test. When you face these choices, you are now equipped with the skillset to weigh the importance of the test versus the significance of the social event. Boom! Decision made!

Some scenarios we face in life require decisions around time management, such as the decision about afterschool clubs that we discussed above. We often have to determine how to maximize our time in our hectic lives. As we get older, these time management decisions will have an even more significant impact on our lives. For example, deciding to take a vacation during a non-busy versus a busy season at work can be life-altering. Overcommitting to too many outside activities and hobbies could increase our stress rather than provide enjoyment.

As discussed earlier in this book, other decisions will revolve around our finances. Do we want to save our allowance or spend it on a new video game we have been eyeing? Some financial decisions will create a significant impact on our lives. Do we want to live in a house or an apartment? Do we want to live in a bustling city or a small town? Will we go to the grocery every week or eat out every night? These decisions have a significant impact on our budgets and how we choose to live our lives.

Some decisions that we make involve our relationships. Do we confront a friend who upset us, or do we let it slide? Do we make amends with our sister after a difficult dialogue at the dinner table last week? Are we going to reach out to the person who isn't pulling their weight on the group project due later this month? Every potential choice comes with its advantages and disadvantages.

When faced with difficult decisions regarding relationships, remember to take a non-emotional approach when necessary. If you need time to calm down before deciding how to respond, take that time. Evaluate your feelings and try to empathize with the other person. How might they be feeling, too? You will also want to consider the seriousness of the situation and how your decision will impact the quality of your relationship over time.

Look for opportunities to practice informed decision-making in the world around you in areas such as academics, finances, and relationships. Opportunities are rich for practice all around you every day!

THE ROLE OF VALUES IN DECISION-MAKING

Every sailor has a guiding star. For you, your guiding star is your set of personal values and beliefs. These values and beliefs play a critical role in the decision-making process.

For example, let's say that honesty is a substantial value for you. If this is the case and you allow honesty to be like your North Star, you will probably more readily admit when you've made a mistake. It will be important to you to apologize and mend the relationship. When you choose between being accountable, lying, or placing blame, you will most likely select honesty and accountability. Those values help you decide based on what matters most to you.

Understanding your values can guide your decisions and help you live a life that aligns closely with who you are as a person. If you value helping others, you might choose to spend your free time volunteering at a local food pantry rather than shopping at the mall. If you value time alone to rest and recharge, the schedule you create for yourself might reflect the necessity of that time.

Values can also help you make tough decisions. Let's say you value your mental health. Unfortunately, you also have a lot of responsibilities on your plate. You joined a new club at school, play several sports, and are involved in your church's youth group. This activity level isn't leaving you much time for homework, and you are falling behind academically. This leaves you stressed, and the lack of sleep at night isn't helping. You have felt agitated and emotional the past few weeks.

Since you value your mental health, you might identify that some things in your schedule aren't working to your advantage. You look at your options and realize that you need to cut at least one activity to give you breathing space in your week. You decide it isn't the best time to join a new club. That gives you two afternoons back each week to dedicate to your academics. Your core value helped you make a difficult decision that worked best for you! Your values serve as your moral compass, guiding you through stormy seas.

Before we wrap up the chapter, it's time for one more treat. It's time to . . . Ask the Captain!

Ask the Captain: Your Decision-Making Questions Divulged

Ask the Captain

Captain, how can I tell if I'm making a truly informed decision or just going with the flow?
Ahoy, shipmate! This one is tricky! Getting caught up and just going with the flow can be so easy. The key here is to gather information about your decision and weigh the pros and cons. Ask yourself if you have thoroughly researched and considered each choice's consequences. If you can explain why you're choosing a particular path, your decision is likely informed!

Captain, what should I do if I am torn between two decisions and can't decide?

Arrr, indecision is like a ship caught in the doldrums! You really can toss and turn about! When you are stuck between a few options and can't seem to decide, seek guidance from sailors you trust. Discuss your options out loud and consider the long-term impact of your choice. Remember, the right choice is not always going to be immediately apparent.

Still need help? Don't forget about that list of pros and cons. If both options yield similar results, don't put too much additional pressure on your choice.

How can I handle the pressure of making big decisions, such as determining my career path?

Navigating the pressure of big decisions can certainly be daunting, me lad! First, remember to break the decision down into smaller tasks. Explore your interests, then gather additional information. Consider the options available to you based on what you find. Don't be afraid to change course; remember that not all decisions must be permanent. Many a captain has changed course over the years and are still successful at what they do.

Captain, what role do values play in decision-making, and how do I know my values?

Remember that values are like your guiding stars, matey! They help you stay true to your course. To discover your values, reflect on what matters to you most. Honesty? Loyalty? Adventure? Something else? Your values will light the way and steer you toward decisions that align with your true self.

How do I know whether to follow my heart or listen to logic when making a difficult decision?

Balancing heart and reason is a bit like navigating between rocky shoals. The truth is, you have to listen to both, matey. Consider your emotions and your rational thoughts. Sometimes, that blend of both will set your course straight. Trust your instincts, but also consider sound information and advice.

As we navigate the chapters of life, understanding the art of informed decision-making will serve as a guiding star. We adjust our course with each choice, charting a path that defines our voyage. So, my fellow sailors, prepare your compass and trust your instincts. The sea of possibilities awaits.

The North Star's Guiding Light (Key Chapter Takeaways)

- Informed decisions empower you to take control of your life and future.
- Consider the long-term benefits and consequences of your choices.
- Effective decision-making involves identifying options, evaluating them, and making a choice.
- When making difficult decisions, prioritize your choices and break them into manageable parts to reduce stress.
- Seek advice from trusted advisors when necessary and give yourself permission to make mistakes.
- Your personal values serve as your moral compass and guide your decisions. Reflect on what matters most to you to discover your values.

Helping to Power the Lighthouse

"Man must behave like a lighthouse; he must shine day and night for the goodness of everyman."

— MEHMET MURAT ILDAN

I know how it feels at this stage of life, with adulthood right around the corner and the turbulent seas making the journey seem so difficult. It feels like you're the only one in need of a lighthouse... No one's talking about their worries and fears, and it seems like everywhere you look, everyone else has it all figured out.

I promise you, they don't. Every one of your classmates is battling the same waters of anxiety and self-doubt as you are – whether they talk about it or not.

Every teenager needs the warm, guiding light of a lighthouse to follow, and I'll let you in on a secret: Most adults do too! But we don't like to ask for help, especially during our teenage years when it's important to most people to make it look like they know what they're doing.

But the internet is full of teens desperately googling for answers, searching for the exact guidance you're getting here, so I'd like to ask you to help me power the lighthouse.

By leaving a review of this book on Amazon, you'll make it easier for those young people to find what they're looking for; you'll make this lighthouse shine its light even brighter.

Reviews make it easier for people to find the information they're looking for… and trust me, you're not alone. There are thousands of teenagers quietly hunting for this information. You can help them find it!

Thank you so much for your support. Now, let's continue our voyage!

Scan the QR code to leave a review!

6

BECOMING A SOLUTION-FINDER: A TEEN'S GUIDE TO PROBLEM-SOLVING

I n our lives, problems are inevitable. Just as we can't always predict the weather at sea, we also can't always predict when problems will arise. Becoming a solution-finder is a way to address problems to the best of our ability. The good news is this chapter will help us do just that!

UNDERSTANDING THE PROBLEM: THE FIRST STEP TO FINDING SOLUTIONS

Just as a sea captain navigates treacherous waters, we also learn that recognizing and identifying problems is the first crucial step in charting a course to safety in our lives. For example, have you ever struggled with balancing schoolwork and a part-time job? The waves of responsibilities seem to be crashing around you, threatening to capsize your world. Before you can set sail towards a solution, however, you must identify the problem's source. As sea captains can't navigate appropriately without understanding the dangers lurking beneath the waves, you can't solve a problem effectively without recognizing its root cause.

In other words, sailors, recognizing that there is a problem and identifying the issue is a critical first step in resolving it!

So, what happens next? In this example, we know we have an issue with time management. First, we need to define the problem clearly and precisely. For example, in the previous scenario, we might be tempted to say, "I'm always busy." Case closed. But what does "I'm always busy" really mean? Perhaps we might say instead, "I'm working four nights during the school week, and I do not have time to study when I get home because I am tired." Now, that is a well-defined problem that we can solve!

Remember, a well-defined problem becomes your North Star, guiding your search for solutions through even the darkest nights!

GENERATING SOLUTIONS: THE POWER OF BRAINSTORMING

Picture this: You're out at sea, surrounded by waves of endless blue. It's smooth sailing until suddenly you are faced with a challenge. Your main mast becomes damaged. At this moment, you have to gather your sailors together to brainstorm a quick solution, just as you should when tackling your own problems on shore.

Brainstorming is like your ship's crew huddled together during a storm, sharing their ideas freely and passionately. At this point, no idea is too wild! The goal is to let your creativity flow like the ocean's currents.

Free thinking helps generate a range of possible solutions to our problems! When we are brainstorming, though, sometimes our ideas can become overwhelming. You can use apps like MindMeister or Trello to organize your ideas visually.

During the brainstorming process, it is essential to remember to take your time with a solution. Like a skilled sailor examining the sky for signs of bad weather, take the time to explore all possibilities.

Need help with the brainstorming process? There are several resources available to help! For example, books like *Six Thinking Hats* by Edward de Bono can provide strategies for effective brainstorming.

Finally, don't forget to discuss your ideas with family, friends, or other trusted adults! The more people you involve in your decision-making processes, the more perspectives you will have that you may not have even considered! Let them be the lighthouse guiding you towards new and better horizons as you find workable solutions for your problems.

EVALUATING OPTIONS: MAKING THE RIGHT CHOICE

After brainstorming, we must evaluate each potential solution and consider its outcomes. Like a sea captain, we need to assess the options before us with a discerning eye when solving problems. After a vigorous brainstorming session, we need to weigh the pros and cons of each solution, just as captains consider how to navigate dangerous waters ahead.

Fortunately, there are tools available to help. Have you ever heard of a SWOT analysis? A SWOT allows us to examine our strengths, weaknesses, opportunities, and threats. It's a trusty navigation chart! What are the strengths and weaknesses of each solution? What opportunities might each one bring, and what threats might they pose? Sailors have to weigh the potential short and long-term effects of their course of action, just as you should with your solutions.

Let's use the problem presented earlier in this chapter as an example of how we might create a SWOT analysis. You work four nights a week and fall behind in your studies. There is a time management issue at hand. You have brainstormed various solutions, including working less and studying at different daily intervals. Let's do a SWOT analysis on each.

	Strengths	Weaknesses	Opportunities	Threats
Work less	More time to study. Reduced fatigue and increased energy. Improved ability to focus academically. Greater work-life balance.	Reduced income. Potential financial stress. Employer may not agree to fewer hours. Potential to limit future workable hours.	Explore part-time jobs that better fit academic needs. Pursue internships or volunteer work related to interests. Time to develop additional skills to enhance future career opportunities.	Financial stress due to reduced income. Competition for different part-time job opportunities. Negative impact on current job performance or professional reputation. Potential strain on relationships with colleagues or supervisors.
Studying at different daily intervals	Flexibility to adapt a study schedule to personal preferences. Ability to accommodate work shifts and other commitments. Ability to break up study sessions, improving retention of information. Potential for better time management and improved productivity.	Requires strong self-discipline and time management skills. Could cause irregular sleep patterns. Potential disruption from external factors beyond your control (noise levels during lunch, etc.). Balancing work and study may still be challenging if work hours are inflexible.	Possibility to participate in extracurricular opportunities or other social events. Enhanced adaptability and resilience due to managing a non-standard study schedule. Chance to collaborate with classmates with similar schedules.	Difficulty maintaining a consistent routine, which can lead to procrastination. Potential negative impact on physical and mental health due to irregular sleep patterns. Reduced access to resources, such as peers and teachers due to unconventional study hours. Risk of isolation from family and friends with traditional schedules.

Ultimately, the choice between these two solutions will depend on you. Do you need financial stability, or is job flexibility more important? Are you disciplined enough to maintain a non-traditional study schedule? Combining both approaches or seeking guidance from academic advisors and mentors could also provide a more balanced solution to the problem at hand.

Remember to be flexible and think outside the box. The sea of possibilities for any problem is always vast. Explore it entirely to find the best route to your desired destination!

IMPLEMENTING THE SOLUTION: TURNING IDEAS INTO ACTION

After carefully considering your options, it's time to take action! A sea captain doesn't just plot a course of action but also must steer the ship forward from the storm. Similarly, you must turn your solution into action, too!

First, break your solution into manageable steps, just as sailors break down complex maneuvers into precise movements. There are project management apps, such as Asana or Trello, to help! These apps allow you to chart your progress in various ways, ensuring you stay on course.

Remember that things could still go wrong, even with a great action plan. We may need to adjust to shifting winds or unexpected storms. Be prepared and know that you must adapt and adjust your strategy as needed. Good sailors do that all the time!

Finally, monitor the results of your solutions closely. For example, if your grades improve after you start spending more time studying, it's a sign that your solution is working in your favor! But if not, don't be disheartened. Just as sailors change their course when necessary, you can adapt a different approach until you find the solution that works for you!

REFLECTING ON THE PROBLEM-SOLVING PROCESS: LEARNING FROM EXPERIENCE

Every journey at sea teaches us a valuable lesson, just as every problem-solving experience brings an opportunity to learn. Reflecting on our journeys and processes is like examining maps and charts after a voyage. It makes us more insightful and prepares us for future challenges.

Keep a journal of your problem-solving experiences. Reflect on what went well and what could be improved, just as a captain logs their observations and experiences at sea. This reflection will help you develop better problem-solving skills over time.

Remember, problem-solving is a journey, not a destination. Every problem you encounter in life is an opportunity to learn and grow. Embrace the journey and keep improving your problem-solving skills. Even captains have to continuously refine their skills to navigate ever-changing seas.

And speaking of captains, we have one to address your most common problem-solving questions! Let's go ahead and ask him what he thinks!

Ask the Captain: Your Answers to Life's Toughest Problem-Solving Questions

Ask the Captain

Dear Captain, how do I recognize when I have a problem? How will I know?

Ahoy, young shipmate! Spotting a problem is like spotting a storm on the horizon! It's essential to do but easy to miss if we aren't paying attention. Remember our chat about emotional intelligence and being self-aware? Self-awareness is one of the key ways we recognize a problem on the horizon of our lives. When you tune into your feelings, look for signs of discomfort and unease. Those are usually the first signs that something is wrong.

A problem may also be identified when you experience a series of obstacles one after another. If you find this happening, stop to think about why these obstacles are occurring. It could be a sign of a problem with something in your life.

Finally, you might see a problem pop up as you evaluate your goals. A barrier may keep appearing between your reality and the completion of your plan. Examine the why behind it and identify if a problem needs to be solved.

Ahoy, Captain! I have a problem, but I have no idea where to start to tackle it. That's why I have a problem in the first place, right?

I can feel your agony, young shipmate! When we have a problem, it can be hard to figure out how to tackle it. After all, if we knew how to avoid it, we probably would have. Remember that brainstorming can lead us to creative solutions to problems we identify. I use my shipmates to do this all the time! When you're stuck, there is nothing wrong with gathering a crew you trust to help you get the problem solved! Sit around and have everyone generate a list of potential solutions. Then, use the SWOT process to evaluate each one!

But what do I do if we find a solution, and I implement it, and it still doesn't work out?
Don't get discouraged, mate! This is bound to happen occasionally, even after an intensive SWOT analysis of the options we brainstormed independently and with our crew! Know that we will always have to adjust our sails with the changing of the wind. It can happen at any time, lad! Be flexible, return to your SWOT analysis, and look at other solutions if the first one doesn't work out. Remember, sometimes the best solution is a combination of a few! Adapt and try a different track. Every setback is a lesson to be learned that will help you on your voyage ahead.

How do I stay motivated to overcome the hard times when my problems seem so big?
Arrr! This is a tough one, lad! When our problems are big and carry heavy emotions, it can be challenging to stay the course, even with a good solution in place. We must keep our goals in sight like a lighthouse in the distance. Remember to break your journey into manageable parts, setting mini milestones and goals to accomplish. This makes the problem seem more manageable and solutions easier to implement as we chart a course toward our goals. Track your progress by checking off each milestone as you go. When you feel you are progressing, it is easier to stay motivated despite the obstacles at hand.

Captain, is there a way to become a better problem-solver?
Like anything in life, practice makes perfect, me laddie! To ensure you are evolving to be a better problem-solver, don't forget to reflect on your journey. Keep a journal of your problem-solving experiences and learn from your mistakes. You'll undoubtedly grow wiser with each voyage.

In the vast sea of life, mastering problem-solving techniques is your compass, your lighthouse, and your guiding light leading you through the fog of uncertain times. With each problem you solve and reflect upon, you become a better sailor on the voyage of life.

The North Star's Guiding Light (Key Chapter Takeaways)

- Problems in life are inevitable. Learning to be a solution-finder equips us to tackle challenges more effectively.
- Recognizing and identifying the problem is the first step in solving it.
- Clearly and explicitly defining a problem is crucial. A well-defined problem becomes your guiding star, leading you toward appropriate solutions.
- Brainstorming allows you to explore all potential solutions. Use people you trust to increase answers and gain ideas through fresh perspectives.
- Evaluate potential solutions through a SWOT analysis, which allows you to consider each option's strengths, weaknesses, opportunities, and threats to make informed decisions.
- Implement the solution by breaking it into manageable steps. Don't forget to track your progress and journal as you reflect upon the results.
- Remember that challenges will arise. It is okay to adjust your approach.

7

BODY AND MIND: UNDERSTANDING PHYSICAL AND MENTAL HEALTH

This time, our lighthouse is beaconing us toward a journey of greater physical and mental health. After all, caring for those aspects of our lives is a critical step toward greater self-reliance and overall well-being.

Paying attention to our physical and mental health keeps us strong throughout our life journey. Good health involves understanding the importance of a balanced diet, regular exercise, adequate sleep, and stress management techniques. We will break down each of these concepts in the sections that follow.

THE POWER OF GOOD NUTRITION

As you begin your journey through life's unchartered waters, it is essential to consider that your body and mind are your vessels - the strong ships that will get you through anything on the vast sea of life! Vessels don't maintain themselves, though. A healthy body and mind require constant care and attention, starting with a healthy diet!

The foundation of any strong ship is good nutrition. Just as the right wind helps power our sails, the right food fuels our bodies. Many factors contribute to good nutrition. Let's break them down now.

- **Maintaining a healthy diet.** To maintain a well-built ship, we must consume a balanced diet rich in fruits, vegetables, lean protein, and whole grains. Consult the United States Department of Agriculture for a food pyramid that will be your trusty chart in the vast sea of dietary choices. It will help you make the right ones!
- **Avoid junk food.** Like the siren maidens of the sea, sugary foods and drinks will call! They may seem tempting, but they have little nutritional value and can lead to weight gain and other health problems. Hydrating with water infused with fresh fruits, such as strawberries and lemons, is better than sugary drinks. Opt for snacks that are fruit and veggie-based, too!
- **Cook at home.** Eating out can be tempting, especially when our lives are busy. Take the helm in the galley by choosing to cook at home, which provides you with control over ingredients and portion sizes. Some websites, such as BBC Good Food, offer quick and healthy recipes crafted specifically for young sailors such as yourselves!

- **Learn to decipher food labels.** Just as sea captains rely on nautical charts, food labels help us make informed decisions about what we eat. The U.S. Food and Drug Administration (FDA) provides a comprehensive guide. Additionally, apps like Fooducate can assist us in decoding labels and rating the nutritional value of the foods we buy.
- **Stay hydrated.** Being well-hydrated is one of the most important things we can do for our bodies. The National Academies of Sciences, Engineering, and Medicine recommends that individuals aged fourteen through eighteen consume between ten and fourteen cups of water daily. Carry a refillable water bottle, like a Hydro Flask or a S'well, to make it easier to stay hydrated throughout the day.

FITNESS FIRST: THE ROLE OF EXERCISE

Along with solid nutrition, we also have to consider the elements of fitness and the role of exercise in our lifelong journey. There are many tips and tricks regarding exercise to keep our sailors fit at sea!

First, daily activity is critical to keep our ship in top-notch shape! The American Heart Association recommends at least sixty minutes of moderate to vigorous daily activity. While that can seem like a lot, consider it training your crew (your body and mind) to handle any challenges that come your way!

Fortunately, there are a lot of digital tools and online resources that can help us keep physically fit. We have access to a treasure trove of fitness resources! Fitness influencers like Rebecca Louise offer beginner-friendly workout videos on YouTube, while mobile apps like Apple Health, Nike Training Club, and MyFitnessPal can track your progress and motivate you to keep physically fit!

Exercise can also influence the way we sleep. Just as a well-rested crew is essential for a smooth voyage, regular exercise helps maintain healthy sleep patterns necessary for our growth and development. Physical activity improves the quality and duration of sleep, as suggested by the National Sleep Foundation (Pacheco, 2013).

Finally, exercise also boasts several mental health benefits. Exercise isn't just for our bodies - it's for our minds, too! Regular exercise releases endorphins, which serve as natural mood lifters. This can be particularly helpful during stressful times, such as prepping for final exams. By improving the quality of our sleep, exercise also helps with another critical aspect of our mental health.

BREAKING DOWN THE BASICS OF MENTAL HEALTH

Now that the strength of your hull has increased, let's dig a bit deeper into our exploration of mental health. Mental health can be tricky to understand, so let's start with a quick definition.

Mental health includes your emotional, psychological, and social well-being. It affects how you think, feel, and act. It's essential to realize that mental health problems are common and nothing to be ashamed of. Celebrities like Selena Gomez and Demi Lovato have openly discussed their struggles, breaking the pre-existing stigma.

Unfortunately, adolescence is a time when many mental health issues begin to emerge. According to the National Institute of Mental Health, nearly 50% of all lifetime mental illnesses begin by age fourteen. That's a lot, isn't it, sailors? Think of this time as a challenging sea to navigate. If you feel yourself struggling, it's okay. We are here to equip you with the knowledge and support needed to weather this intense storm.

SPOTTING COMMON MENTAL HEALTH PROBLEMS AMONG TEENS

Just like on the waves of stormy seas, knowledge is our anchor in recognizing and addressing common mental health issues among teens. Let's review a few and see if you recognize these challenges in people you may know, love, or even in yourself.

Anxiety Disorders: Anxiety disorders often function like turbulent seas. They can include panic attacks, post-traumatic stress disorder, and phobias. Signs of these anxiety disorders could consist of:

- Dip in academic performance
- Loss of interest in activities that used to be enjoyable
- Decrease in social interactions
- Negative self-talk, such as "I can't do this" or "I'm not good at anything"
- Increased negativity about life and/or others
- Insomnia

- Increased exhaustion for no reason
- Loss of appetite or eating disorders
- Changes in mood and behavior
- Substance abuse
- Increase in risky behaviors
- Avoidance of people, places, and things that trigger anxious feelings

Depression: Depressive feelings include persistent sadness and lack of interest in activities that used to be enjoyed. It can feel like a real anchor weighing you down. Common signs of depression in teens can include:

- Sadness
- Anxiety
- Lack of energy and/or motivation
- Temper outbursts or episodes of violence
- Becoming easily irritable
- Sleeping excessively
- Sleeping insufficiently
- Little or no appetite
- Excessive eating
- Withdrawal from people you love
- Loss of interest in activities that used to be enjoyable
- Irrational fear
- Lack of concentration
- Poor memory
- Increased substance use/abuse
- Poor academic performance
- Skipping school

- Being self-patronizing or critical
- Feelings of helplessness*
- Feelings that things will never improve*
- Increased commentary about death or dying*
- Threatening suicide*

When four or more of these depressive symptoms are observed and occur for more than two weeks, it is recommended to seek professional support. If any of the last four symptoms are observed, help should be sought immediately for yourself or others.

Eating disorders: Body issues are also common during the teenage years and they can trigger eating disorders, such as anorexia, bulimia, or binge eating. The symptoms of each disorder can be unique.

- **Anorexia:** drastic weight loss, dressing in layers to hide weight loss, preoccupation with weight, food, calories, and dieting, excessive exercising
- **Bulimia:** evidence of eating large quantities of food, evidence of purging (frequent bathroom trips, smells of vomiting, etc.), calluses on the back of hands from self-induced vomiting, dental problems (enamel erosion, cavities, discoloration, etc.)
- **Binge eating:** eating large quantities of food in secret, feelings of disgust, depression, and guilt after overeating, stealing/hoarding food

Although these mental health disorders can be intimidating and scary, the National Institute of Mental Health provides detailed resources and guides for these disorders and how to seek help. Just as captains on the high seas rely on their charts and navigational tools for support, you can rely on these resources to steer your course when these symptoms are identified in yourself or those you love.

MASTERING STRESS MANAGEMENT TECHNIQUES

Unfortunately, like unpredictable weather at sea, stress is a part of life. Learning to manage it is essential to our overall well-being and our ability to cope with stressors that pop up throughout the day in an emotionally intelligent way.

There are several ways that we can manage stress. For example, we can utilize specific stress-reduction techniques to mitigate or lessen it. Deep breathing, progressive muscle relaxation, and visualization can all help to reduce stress. Apps like Calm or Insight Timer offer guided meditations tailored to these needs. A voice will walk you through strategies for different breathwork or inform you how to complete a body scan where you relax each set of muscles from your head to your feet. Check out what's available to you when you aren't under stress so you already have the tools in your toolbox when a stressful event occurs.

Creative outlets are also great ways to take a break from stress. Whether painting, playing music, or even coding if you're into math, these activities are like safe harbors amid uncontrollable storms.

Physical activity is also a way to lessen daily stress in our lives. Regular physical activity is a powerful stress reliever; it doesn't have to be strenuous to be effective, either! Activities such as yoga, tai chi, or walking can help calm the turbulent seas of stress.

Using creative outlets and engaging in physical activity are proactive and reactive ways to respond to stress in our environments. When we allow creativity to flow and move our bodies, we create feel-good hormones that mitigate the impact of stress.

Do you ever feel obligations and responsibilities pile up on your plate and start to get a sense of being overwhelmed? It could be that you don't have an effective time management plan. Like charting a course through tricky waters, managing your time effectively, prioritizing tasks, and taking breaks when needed can prevent stress from piling up. Apps like Todoist can help you stay organized if you struggle to do so alone. The next time you start to feel overwhelmed, stop and ask yourself if you have an effective time management plan.

During stress, it is also helpful for us to maintain a positive social network. Although stress can make us want to withdraw, your ship's crew matters! Positive relationships with family and friends can provide emotional support when the seas get rough and create a sense of belonging, too! Joining clubs or organizations that serve a good cause can also expand your social circles, create a sense of giving back and purpose, and foster a sense of community. These are all essential characteristics in times of increased stress.

Finally, we should mention the importance of effective communication during stress before ending this section. When we communicate effectively and assertively, we can manage interpersonal conflicts better, reducing social pressure. Role-playing scenarios can help us practice these communication skills, just like sailors at sea practice effective navigation techniques.

We have a variety of stress-reduction techniques we can implement both before and during times of stress to mitigate its impact on our lives. Learning proper stress reduction techniques, staying creative, getting physically active, effectively managing our time, maintaining a positive social network, and effectively communicating with those around us can all lessen stress in critical times.

EMBRACING THE POWER OF SELF-CARE

We also can't forget the value of self-care in our daily lives. It's part of maintaining robust physical and mental health. And remember, self-care is not selfish. It's necessary for maintaining strong mental health. Here are some self-care techniques to mitigate stress and continually keep our minds and bodies strong.

- **Engage in activities you enjoy.** Activities you enjoy are natural stress relievers. Find what works for you, whether it's listening to your favorite music, watching a movie, reading a book, painting, or even journaling. Indulge in it! Your mental health will thank you!

- **Maintain a regular sleep schedule.** Establishing a normal sleep routine is one way to steer your ship toward success. Teens are recommended to sleep between eight and ten hours each night. Create a routine that allows for deep sleep to occur. Shut off devices an hour before bed and create a relaxing pre-bedtime routine. Take a bath or a shower, journal, or read. Whatever you do, create a calming atmosphere conducive to solid sleep.
- **Eat a well-balanced diet.** As quality materials maintain a ship, nutritious foods fuel your body and mind. Remember, apps such as Fooducate are available to help you make healthy eating choices. If you are shopping for healthy foods, try to stick to the outer edges of the grocery store. This is where you will find your fruits, vegetables and fresh products, whereas the aisles typically contain processed foods that are less healthy.
- **Seek help when needed.** Don't hesitate to reach out for help when you need it. If you feel overwhelmed, talk to a trusted adult, counselor, or even a helpline, such as Teen Line. Remember, even a sea captain needs a navigator from time to time.

Embrace the power of self-care as a natural part of your daily life. Once you establish these routines as a part of your day-to-day, you will feel healthier and more robust in your body and mind.

SUPPORTING MENTAL HEALTH ONLINE

We can't end the chapter on physical and mental health without discussing one of the most influencing factors on our well-being - our online activities. In this digital age, we must be cautious to evaluate our behaviors both on and offline.

When online, be mindful of social media use. How much time are you spending online each day? How are you using social media in a positive manner, such as by posting about upcoming volunteering events or strengthening your digital footprint in a beneficial way? Or are you negatively impacting your self-esteem and mental health by constantly comparing yourself with others? Remember, what you see on social media is like the freshly polished exterior of a ship. It looks good but doesn't reveal everything inside. Don't be fooled by what a video or post fails to show!

Do you find yourself struggling with inappropriate social media use? We can also use the internet to support us in that arena positively! Seek support from online communities, such as TeensHealth. Websites like this offer advice on various topics to guide you toward more appropriate social media use. Some forums, like ReachOut, let you connect with other teens facing similar issues. Just as you rely on your ship's crew, these communities can provide support and guidance along your path.

Finally, always remember to stand up against cyberbullying and never participate in it. Cyberbullying can have severe effects on your mental health. Do not stay silent if you are being bullied or observe someone else being bullied. Please report it to the social media platform and talk to a trusted adult. We must all stand up against rough seas to protect our fellow sailors.

And now, let's finish this part of our journey with another edition of Ask the Captain!

Ask the Captain: All You Want to Know about Physical and Mental Health

Ask the Captain

Ahoy, Captain! I know I need to steer a healthy ship. But there is so much to think about when it comes to being healthy. What should my top priorities be?

Well, shipmate, this is a great question to ask indeed! Unfortunately, there is no correct answer that is going to work for everyone on deck. Health can be a very personal journey, but there are some basic things to consider to help you along the way!

First, consider your sleep schedule. Regularly sleeping eight to ten hours each night will improve your mental health. Being well-rested helps you navigate stressful events in emotionally intelligent ways.

Next, it's all about what you eat! Try to stick to fresh foods, such as fruits and vegetables, lean meats, and anything you find around the outer edge of a grocery store. Avoid those inner aisles and processed foods that contain too many sugars to help you on your path.

Additionally, we can't forget about the power of exercise, lad! Daily movement is vital to producing the feel-good hormones we need to tackle stress and stay healthy from day to day.

Finally, find a stress management plan that works for you. When you get into a stressful situation, you need some tools in your toolbox to get you through. Whether you regularly meditate and journal or practice a hobby you love, knowing what fuels your spirit will help you stay in optimal health.

I feel like so many people around me struggle with their mental health, Captain. Is it normal and how can I help?

Unfortunately, laddie, if you see someone around you who seems to be struggling, it's probably because they are. Nearly 50% of all lifetime mental illnesses begin by age fourteen. It's good to look for signs that someone is struggling, such as sudden changes in mood, diet, and other daily routines. If you suspect someone you know or love is struggling, seek help in the form of a trusted adult. Remember, no one needs to struggle in silence. Not you or anyone else you love!

Ahoy, Captain! I've heard about self-care, but it seems expensive and I don't even have a job! What can I do to take care of myself?

Self-care is essential, young sailor. But there is good news. It doesn't have to cost a thing! While social media may project the idea that we have to go to a spa or take a trip to engage in self-care, the most important forms of self-care happen right here at home! Self-care is as simple as caring for your body and mind in ways that feel good! That could be by YouTubing a yoga class, following a guided meditation, or just making sure you're eating and sleeping well each day. Don't overcomplicate the process. Solid self-care can be as simple as creating a life-giving routine that works for you each day!

How do I cope with normal stress and hardship when everything is on social media?

Ahoy, young sailor! Sailing through the modern seas of social media can make the waters rocky! The Captain is here to help you through the chaotic seas of stress that come amidst the ever-present digital storm.!

1. **Chart your own course.** First, remember that you are a captain chartering your course! Just like a boat captain plots a clear routecourse before a sail, you can also establish boundaries for your social media use. Set limits on screen time and determine who you allow to navigate alongside you. Follow those who fill your bucket with sunshine while, unfollowing negativity and anyone who threatens to throw your course off track.

2. **Mindfully anchor.** When the storms of social media are swirling around you and the ocean threatens to take you under its claws, practice mindfully anchoring. Take a break from social media to reconnect with the real world. It's just like dropping an anchor in a calm bay to regain your bearings.

3. **Virtual ship maintenance.** Just like a ship's hull needs regular care, so does your online presence! It is critical to ensure that your online presence reflects your true self. Curate your social media profiles to showcase your best qualities, including your current missions and interests. Volunteer? Showcase a recent community contribution. Applying for a big scholarship? Talk about what most excites you about your ideal school. When you post positive information about yourself and your life, you will attract more positivity to you!

4. **Ride the waves of compassion.** Everyone battles imposter syndrome or the feeling of inadequacy with regard to social media. Show compassion and empathy in your online community. Remember, everyone is sailing their own sea. Model the love and compassion you want others to show you! Again, put out positivitye and positivitye comes back to you!

5. **Check for navigational accuracy.** Not all information you come across on social media will be accurate, just like sometimes the weather forecast can be a tad bit off on the high seas! Don't let false or misleading posts steer you off course. Check the facts!

6. **Be present on the water.** Instead of mindlessly scrolling social media and falling into a bottomless pit, practice presence. Engage in meaningful conversations with like-minded individuals, listen actively, and use the platforms to connect with others.

7. **Prioritize adventures.** No one wants to get on a boat and then sit under the deck, scrolling social media when there are sunsets to chase! Prioritize your real-life adventures over digital ones. Spend time with those you love, practice your hobbies, and pursue your passions beyond the screen!

8. **Know when to sail away.** Remember, logging off and taking a break from social media is okay when it becomes too overwhelming. In fact, it's recommended to take a break at various times during the day and on certain days of the week! Take the time to rest and recharge your utmost treasure - your mental well-being.

It may seem like the seas of social media are uncharted, but never forget that you steer the ship! You have the power to navigate the seas wisely. Keep a steady hand on the helm and a clear course in mind.

As you continue your journey through life's unpredictable seas, always remember to keep your ship - both body and mind - in the best possible condition. The voyage may be challenging, but with the knowledge and practices outlined in this chapter, you'll be well-prepared to navigate any waters that come your way!

The North Star's Guiding Light (Key Chapter Takeaways)

- Your mind and body are like vessels sailing through life's seas. Keep them strong by maintaining a balanced diet rich in fruits, vegetables, lean protein, and whole grains.
- Avoid junk food as much as possible. Opt for healthy snacks and hydrate with water (on average, about twelve cups daily). Learn to decipher food labels to help you make healthy food choices.
- Aim to exercise at least sixty minutes each day. Moderate to vigorous exercise is best.
- Quality sleep greatly influences physical and mental health. Aim for eight to ten hours each night.
- Anxiety disorders, depression, and eating disorders are common among teens. Recognize signs and seek support when needed.
- Stress-reduction techniques help reduce daily stress. Deep breathing, meditation, physical activity, effective time management, and maintaining positive relationships are all ways to mitigate stress.
- Self-care is essential to mental and physical health. Engage in activities you enjoy, maintain a regular sleep schedule, eat a balanced diet, and don't hesitate to seek help when necessary.
- Use social media mindfully. Avoid negative comparisons and seek support when necessary. Remember to stand up against cyberbullying and report incidents when necessary.

8

NO PLACE LIKE HOME: MASTERING BASIC LIFE SKILLS

We have reached the point in our journey where it's time to start navigating the day-to-day! Although it can sometimes seem daunting, it's a necessary task of the seas! In this chapter, we will learn how to navigate those seemingly challenging tasks independently and with ease. Whether it's learning how to do the laundry, cook simple meals, or keep your living space tidy, we have all the tips and tricks you need!

SPIN CYCLE: DEMYSTIFYING THE LAUNDRY PROCESS

You already know it. Those piles of laundry sure do build up fast! To ensure your clothes stay shipshape, here are some laundry basics every good sailor should know:

Sorting Clothes: This sounds pretty basic. But separating your whites from your colors can avoid a tie-dye disaster no one wants! Consider finding a hamper with two separate compartments to make the task even easier come laundry time. Toss your lights in one and your darks in the other for a foolproof laundry process. Don't forget to check pockets for forgotten items, too!

Pre-treating Stains: Stains are common; most will come out in the wash. Some, however, require pre-treatment for maximum stain reduction. You can Google some good stain-specific options. Spaghetti stains will come out using different methods than grease.

Choosing the Right Detergent: Choosing a quality detergent can make all the difference in how your clothes fit and feel. In today's market, many options are available, depending on your needs. For example, if you have sensitive skin, labels such as "Free and Clear" may be necessary. If you are hard on your clothes, you might consider something stronger. Dirt and grease stains can be hard to fight, and "Heavy Duty" might be the label for you. Tide and Persil are traditionally highly-ranked choices. If being eco-friendly is important, consider environmentally considerate options, such as Seventh Generation.

Decoding Laundry Symbols: Just as sailors read nautical navigation charts, you also have to decipher laundry symbols on your clothing tags so you don't end up with a sweater that might fit your baby sister after it goes through the wash. Those symbols aren't just random shapes - they are instructions for how to wash your clothes! For instance, a tub symbol with a hand means "hand wash only," while a triangle crossed out means "do not bleach."

Water Temperatures: Different materials require different heat levels to obtain maximum levels of clean. Here are some general guidelines from *Good Housekeeping* to follow when determining which water temperature to use:

- Cotton: Hot, warm, or cool water; high, regular, or low dryer temperature.
- Linen: Cool or warm water; tumble dry low or air dry.
- Nylon: Cool or warm water; medium or low dryer temperature.
- Polyester: Cool or warm water; medium or low dryer temperature.
- Rayon: Cool water; tumble dry low or line dry; hand washing is recommended.
- Silk: Cool or warm water; air, line, or dry flat; hand washing is recommended.
- Spandex: Cool water; line dry.
- Wool: Cool or warm water; tumble dry low or dry flat; hand washing is recommended.

Determining the Spin Cycle: You may have come to the point where it's time to decide which cycle to choose. There are many options, and all have a purpose. Here are some of our best tips for selecting the proper cycle for you:

- Delicates: This cycle has a gentler agitation and slower spin to prevent damage to delicate garments that might otherwise snag or rip.

- Casual or Permanent Press Cycles: These cycles cool the water gradually and have slower spin speeds that minimize wrinkles.
- Stain Cycles: These cycles start cold to keep stains from setting in. Then, they heat up gradually to thoroughly remove stains.
- Bulky Bedding Cycles: These cycles add a second rinse or increase the spin speed to extract more water for heavier blankets and quilts.

Drying Clothes: Immediately place your clothing in the dryer once the wash cycle is complete. If not, you risk clothes becoming damp and smelling foul. Choose the appropriate dryer cycle based on the type of load you have washed, just like above. Use a dryer sheet to keep static to a minimum and leave clothes smelling fresh.

Folding and Putting Away Clothes: When the dryer cycle is complete, fold and put your clothes away right away to avoid wrinkles and the need to rerun the dryer cycle.

Having a scheduled wash day is great for keeping up with laundry. For example, if you always play softball on Tuesday nights, that might be the ideal time to toss your clothes in the wash so stains don't set in. Often have free time on Saturdays? Perhaps that's the day for you! Whatever you choose, having a system can help you avoid large piles of laundry that cause this chore to become an all-day event.

MASTERCHEF JUNIOR: COOKING UP SIMPLE, NUTRITIOUS MEALS

Not only do sailors have to keep up with laundry, but they also need provisions to survive at sea! Here are some tips and tricks for embarking on your first culinary adventures.

Let's start with the most important meal of the day - breakfast! Learn to make scrambled eggs, toast, and a smoothie to kick off your day. Here's how:

- **Scrambled Eggs:** Heat a small amount of butter in a skillet over medium-low heat. While the skillet is warming, crack two eggs in a bowl and scramble them up with a fork. Add a bit of salt and pepper. Once the butter melts, dump the whisked eggs into a skillet and slowly stir for about two minutes. And - voila! Eggs are ready! Add some shredded cheese and an additional minute in the skillet so the cheese can melt.
- **Toast:** It doesn't get any easier than toast! Take a few slices of bread and pop them into the toaster at a temperature of your liking. Add butter, jelly, or jam!
- **Smoothies:** Many good smoothie recipes are available online based on your flavor preferences. For an easy first attempt, try the following: In a blender, combine one frozen banana, one tablespoon of peanut butter, ½ cup of unsweetened Greek yogurt, and 1 cup of unsweetened milk. Blend, and you're done!

Next, it's time to conquer a quick and easy lunch or dinner - pasta! Pasta is a versatile and straightforward dish to master for chefs of all varieties! You can Google many recipes, but typically, you can start by following the boiling instructions on your choice box of pasta. Add a sauce of your flavor preference and you have a meal - usually in ten minutes or less!

As a safety reminder, always turn off the stove and other appliances when not in use. Also, never leave cooking food unattended. There is nothing worse than that water boiling over onto the stove!

As you gain more confidence in the kitchen, Google or ask ChatGPT for additional easy recipes for foods you love. Soon, you'll be grilling burgers, baking casseroles, and maybe even giving a bit of baking a go! The kitchen is your oyster, sailors! Start slow and work your way up the chef's rung!

KEEP IT CLEAN: BASIC HOUSEKEEPING 101

So far, we've got you clothed and fed. But a tidy ship is a happy ship. We all know what it feels like to get a bit behind in keeping our spaces clean. So, why not get a plan to stay ahead of the game? It's time to talk about the basics of Housekeeping 101!

First, we have to commit to some regular cleaning. Although it may not seem like a big deal, preventing the everyday buildup of dirt and clutter around the house will save you time and unnecessary maintenance. Here are a few housekeeping hacks for teens that will help you create a system that will work in your home now and when you first venture out on your own!

- **Decide how much mess you can live with.** It sounds weird, but we all function differently in our environments, depending on our surroundings. Some people function well with a bit of clutter, while others have to maintain a spotless home to thrive. Determine how much mess you can live with to maximize productivity in your environment.
- **Remove all trash.** When you first start to declutter, it is essential to first remove all garbage. Take a trash bag to the area in need, whether it be your closet, bedroom, bathroom, or additional space. You will find that you can quickly clear clutter that doesn't belong.
- **Make your bed.** This one seems minor, but it is a big mental win for your day! By accomplishing this one task in the morning, you create momentum to knock out additional to-dos throughout the day.
- **Commit to daily decluttering.** Even removing three small items each day can impact your daily routine. We often come home with homework papers, leftover food containers, cups, and more. Committing to decluttering your personal spaces daily eases the cleaning process, reducing the work you must do when it's time to do a deeper cleaning.
- **Put clothes where they belong.** Tossing our clothes on the floor and going straight to bed can be tempting. Unfortunately, this is also how clean clothes we don't put away get thrown back in the wash a second time.

Commit to putting dirty clothes in your hamper and clean clothes in drawers or appropriately hung.

- **Start with larger messes first.** Once you remove trash and clutter from your space, tackle the next most significant project on your list. You may need to clean your messy desk. Perhaps your bathtub has buildup for days. Tackle the largest or most undesirable chore first. The rest will seem more manageable and will go quickly in comparison!
- **Create an organizational system that works for you.** Once you start this process, you will quickly see where your messy habits lie. Are you tired of tackling large piles of laundry? Put a better system in place. Have papers that constantly overrun your desk? Consider a better filing process so your desk isn't always a mess.
- **Deodorize.** Finally, consider a way to make your space smell great. Depending on your preference, various plug-ins, diffusers, and candles can help.

It's also essential to keep a stock of cleaning supplies handy. Just like you need go-to resources in a pinch on a ship, keeping a few cleaning products nearby will make life easier when tackling dirtier tasks. Brands such as Mr. Clean and Clorox offer a range of products, from all-purpose cleaners to scrubbing brushes. If you want more eco-friendly options, those exist, too!

Finally, don't forget to clean some of your most used technology gadgets! Did you know keyboards, phones, and earbuds can harbor more germs than a toilet seat? Gross, huh? Use a microfiber cloth and a gentle cleaner like WHOOSH! for screens.

FRESH AND CLEAN: PERSONAL GROOMING AND HYGIENE PRACTICES

And now, we can't forget about you in this final section about personal grooming and hygiene. Just like sailors need to ward off the damaging salt of the sea, we must keep you clean and presentable, too!

Some of these practices are basic. Start by making sure you shower at least once a day. Consider it like your daily swim in the sea! Regular showering promotes good hygiene and sound sleep, which also has mental and physical health benefits. The same goes for brushing your teeth. Brands such as Dove soap and Colgate toothpaste offer a range of options suitable for teens based on your individual needs.

It's also necessary to consider skincare, just as sailors strive to protect the ship's hull. Although current marketing can be confusing, essential skincare mustn't be overly complex. Consider a simple routine with a cleanser, moisturizer, and sunscreen to protect your skin from those pesky UV rays. CeraVe and Neutrogena are popular and affordable options that will work for most teens.

Finally, remember that mental hygiene is essential, too. This means clearing the mind's clutter, just like you clear clutter in a room! Apps like Headspace and Calm for guided meditations can cleanse your mind and reduce daily stress.

And now, before we put this chapter to bed, let's go ahead and play our favorite trivia game. Let's see if we can stump the captain!

Ask the Captain: Your Basic Life Skills Questions Uncovered

Ask the Captain

Ahoy, Cap'n! I'm sailing into adulthood and need some basic life skills to keep my ship afloat. Do you think you can help?

Of course, laddie! I will be your guiding light! What skills do ye seek?

First, my room is a bit of a mess. I can't ever seem to keep it under control. Can you help?

Oh, mate! That room always seems to be a never-ending chore. I recommend coming up with a daily cleaning process that works for you. For example, have a system for daily garbage disposal and decluttering. Keep a trash can nearby that you can empty regularly, and don't forget to discard any leftover or useless items daily, too. This will keep clutter to a minimum. Then, create a few organizational systems to keep your room tidy each day. You can start with a filing system for leftover papers from school and a way to keep your clothes organized each day, such as investing in a two-compartment hamper and committing to putting clean clothes away immediately after drying. Those are some of my favorite hacks for keeping my bedroom clean!

Speaking of laundry, Cap'n, how do ye keep up with it all?
Oh, shipmate! Laundry can easily be the bane of our existence if we don't have a sound system in place. I recommend separating your dirty clothes into lights and darks as you go and committing to a specific day or time when your laundry will get done each week. Look at your schedule and pick a standard time that may work best. If you often have dirty football uniforms on Fridays, Saturday mornings might be best for you. If you have free time on Wednesday nights, perhaps that's your day!

What about feeding myself, Cap'n? Where do I even start? It's so much easier just to eat out.
Alas, mate! I feel your pain. Although eating out can be convenient when you're a busy teenager, it's also quite expensive. Learning to cook a few simple meals, such as eggs and pasta, can help you save money for the things you want to do. Google a few recipes you love, and commit to starting small. You will expand your repertoire in time!

Although many of these life skills seem simple and basic, not following them can adversely affect your life! Remember, simple processes and procedures for basic daily skills can make our ships sail smoother, especially when the seas get more stressful than we'd like. Keeping systems in place keeps ourselves and our spaces tidy, well-laundered, and fed. A little intention always packs a big punch so we can focus on the more significant details of our worlds.

The North Star's Guiding Light (Key Chapter Takeaways)
• To keep your clothes in the best condition possible, sort, and pre-treat stains, choose the suitable detergent based on your needs, decode laundry symbols for proper washing, and choose the correct water temperatures for different fabrics.
• In the kitchen, start simple with easy recipes such as scrambled eggs and pasta. You can explore more recipes as you gain confidence on your culinary voyage.
• Remove trash, declutter, and put clothes away daily to keep your personal spaces tidy. Tackle larger messes first and create an organizational system that meets your needs.
• Shower daily and brush your teeth twice daily to maintain proper hygiene. Establish a simple skincare routine to keep your skin protected.
• Remember that mental hygiene is a priority, too. Rely on apps such as Headspace and Calm to clear the mental clutter from your head.

9

MASTERING TIME: MAKING EVERY MINUTE COUNT

And so, we meet again, young sailors! As your fearless Captain, I am here to tell you that time is your most precious treasure in the vast ocean of life. Thus, we must learn to navigate the tides of time with wisdom and efficiency, making every minute count! In this chapter, we will dive into the art of time management - a skill that will help you conquer the challenges of school, work, hobbies, and friendships. By mastering time, you'll reduce stress, boost productivity, and find more joyful moments in life! Before we get too far ahead, let's start with the idea of time as the most valuable currency on land!

TIME: THE MOST VALUABLE CURRENCY

Time can be considered the most valuable currency we have. Unlike money, which typically comes to mind when we think of currency, you cannot reclaim it once spent. If we waste or squander it, we don't get it back. Thus, time is the most valuable resource we have!

Let's look back at the way you spent your time today. Take a moment and think back to the moment you woke up. What did you do first? Did you pick up your phone and start scrolling TikTok? Did you hit snooze on your alarm? Did you scramble to get ready because you overslept? Where did your morning hours go? When you were supposed to be studying, did your attention get diverted to Snapchat? At dinner, were you present with family or friends?

On average, we spend over three hours on our phones daily. Do you consider that time well spent?

Teens, just like adults, have choices about how they spend their time. We all have twenty-four hours in a day. It's how we use them that differs. Although we all have basic needs that need to be met, such as showering and grooming, eating, and sleeping, we also have individual needs. Some of us need more time for studying, while others have obligations such as jobs.

So, what skills matter when it comes to managing our time? Here are a few solid places to start:

- **Get your plans out of your head**. By the time we reach high school, we have a lot going on in our lives. There are tests, projects, college applications, clubs, sports, work, and family all vying for our time. All of our responsibilities can easily get jumbled inside our heads! We must get them out of our heads and onto paper to begin organizing our lives.

- **Learn to plan**. Nothing is worse than being midweek and realizing you have lost control of your time. You should have remembered that big book report. You didn't wash your uniform because you didn't write down the date and time of your games. The most successful planners can plan their week in advance. Try to sit down on a Sunday evening and map out your busy week ahead.
- **Efficiency is more important than quantity.** Time management isn't about cramming your day full of tasks from beginning to end. Instead, it's about simplifying how you work, allowing you to accomplish tasks faster, and choosing the right time for each one. For example, if you're a morning person, you might finish homework first thing in the morning, while night owls may prefer to wrap it up before they go to sleep. The time of day affects our analytical capabilities, so plan accordingly.
- **Learn the art of saying no.** It's okay to politely decline an offer when you are overextended or your priorities don't align.

If you've never done it, you may also find it beneficial to track your time. See where your hours go! Try it for a week. Write down every activity you do during the day and how long it takes. Then, categorize your activities, such as studying, sports, or time with friends. You might be surprised at how much "free" time you have or realize that all that TikTok scrolling adds up to a scary amount of time!

THE MAGIC OF PRIORITIZING

A secret magic exists in time management when we prioritize some of our most important tasks. When we can order our tasks based on importance and urgency, we ensure that critical tasks are completed without last-minute stress.

Let's say you have a pretty heavy week at school. You have a science test on Tuesday, a book report due on Thursday, and a significant group project in social studies on Friday. You decide to prioritize the science test since it's the first major academic event of the week and the subject you struggle with the most. Once the test is done, you can focus on your book report and group project, which are easier subjects and require less time to complete.

But how do you decide what is urgent, important, or a combination of the two? The

Eisenhower Box can help!

The Eisenhower Box is named after President Dwight D. Eisenhower, the 34th president of the United States. It helps us prioritize different tasks by creating a matrix like this:

The Eisenhower Matrix		
	Urgent	Not Urgent
Important	*Quadrant 1*	*Quadrant 2*
Not Important	*Quadrant 3*	*Quadrant 4*

- In Quadrant 1, we place tasks that are both important and urgent. These are our highest-priority tasks for the week!
- In Quadrant 2, we place important but not urgent tasks. Deadlines for these may be flexible, or they may not have a timeline.
- Quadrant 3 tasks are not important but are urgent. These are tasks we can often delegate to someone else.
- Quadrant 4 tasks are neither important nor urgent.

To better understand what types of tasks fit where, we must understand the definitions of "urgent" and "important."

Urgent: Tasks that require immediate action.

An example of an urgent task may be a deadline for an assignment at school or making an on-time payment for your credit card.

Important: Tasks that contribute to our long-term goals.

An example of an important task may be regularly exercising or writing a certain number of words each day.

Now, let's look at some examples in each quadrant:

The Eisenhower Matrix		
	Urgent	Not Urgent
Important	• Submit revisions to an assignment I failed that are due today. • Study for tomorrow's science test. • Pay my credit card bill that is due today so I do not incur a late fee.	• Go to the gym when I can fit it into my schedule. • Buy my mom a birthday gift. • Practice the piano.
Not Important	• Feed the dog. • Check email. • Go to the store.	• Watch Netflix. • Download songs on Spotify.

Most of the quadrants are self-explanatory. Our urgent/important tasks take priority, and we must squeeze in Quadrant 2 tasks when we have time. Quadrant 3 is the trickiest one. These are usually daily tasks that must be done, but we can spend too much time on them, tricking ourselves into thinking they are more important than they are. They can usually be delegated (given to someone else) or automated with the help of technology tools. Grocery delivery, anyone?

Also, please don't disregard Quadrant 4. Even though these tasks are neither urgent nor important, they are still part of the necessary downtime our bodies need to recuperate so that we can focus on the urgent/important tasks at hand! Don't neglect Quadrant 4 completely. We all need that rest and rejuvenation now and then!

Now, why don't you give it a try? Brain dump your next list of to-dos and see if you can put them in the Eisenhower Box. Does this help you start prioritizing those essential tasks? It's a great organizational tool. But what do you do when you have your matrix complete? How do you start tackling those urgent/important to-dos? I have a hunch we are about to find out!

MAXIMIZING PRODUCTIVITY WITH TOOLS AND TECHNIQUES

We have learned how to use the Eisenhower Box to prioritize our most urgent and important tasks. But how do we tackle those priorities that fall into Quadrants 1 and 2? It's time to talk about some time management tools we can utilize to organize essential tasks, set reminders, and break large tasks into smaller chunks.

First, let's talk about time management tools. Several apps can help us organize and track our most critical priorities. Here are a few tried and true ones!

- **Google Calendar.** Google Calendar is a great app to schedule and track your tasks. Enter key weekly events into your virtual calendar and set reminders for an appropriate interval ahead of the task/event. For example, if you have a big project due on Thursday, you might set a reminder for Tuesday and Wednesday to work on the task ahead of time. Soccer game on Thursday? Remind yourself to make sure your uniform is clean on Wednesday night.
- **Forest.** Forest is a productivity tool designed to help users stay off their devices when they need to fully

engage in the task at hand. A timer runs down, and a tree or shrub grows with time spent on a task. If you click out of the app to look at something else on your phone, the tree dies.

- **Remember the Milk.** This task-organizing app is helpful for teens who struggle with goal-setting, prioritizing, and time management or organization. Type in the task's name and then organize it according to the kind of task (work, home, school, etc.), priority, due date, and time. Alarm reminders on iOS devices can include a "Moo," "Cowbell," or typical alarm sound.

Fun fact time! Did you know that after every distraction, it can take about twenty-three minutes to recover from interrupted time? Finding ways to limit our distractions packs a big punch! Aside from apps like Forest, there are other techniques we can utilize to intensify our focus and boost our productivity over short periods. Let's explore a few of these now!

TOOLS FOR EFFICIENCY

We can utilize various time management techniques to increase efficiency with our time. Have you ever sat down to study for a test but immediately responded to a Snapchat instead? Or do you start to read and find yourself distracted by something that needs attention in your room? We can become overstimulated not only by our phones but also by our surrounding environment. Thus, we must equip ourselves with tools to overcome our urges to unfocus in order to prolong the task at hand.

Methods such as the Pomodoro Technique, time blocking, or the two-minute rule can help.

The Pomodoro Technique

Did you know that *pomodoro* means "tomato" in Italian? It's true! You may wonder why we are discussing tomatoes as a time management technique. Let's break it down for you now.

The Pomodoro Technique is a focus strategy that requires twenty-five minutes of uninterrupted work followed by a five-minute break. After about four consecutive work cycles, you take longer breaks of fifteen to twenty minutes. Each work interval is called a pomodoro.

Using this technique, you only need a task and a timer to get into a rhythm! Remember those priorities we organized in Quadrants 1 and 2 in our Eisenhower Box? Let's start with a few of those. Pick a task, set the timer for twenty-five minutes, and work until time runs out, or for one pomodoro. Then, take a short break! After your break, tackle another task by setting the timer and starting again!

Most of the time, you will only complete some of your tasks in a twenty-five-minute cycle. For example, let's say you have to write a research report. It's unlikely this is one singular twenty-five-minute task. You may need to chunk this task into several pomodori or cycles. Perhaps one cycle is gathering the research you need to write the report. Another cycle may be creating an outline based on the resources you found. The third cycle could be writing the rough draft; the final cycle may be editing your final product. In just four short pomodori, you have completed the task!

The Pomodoro Technique improves mental agility and reduces the daunting feeling that can come with large tasks. Give it a try the next time you need to conquer a few overwhelming to-dos. You will quickly find a rhythm and an efficiency cycle that feels natural!

Time Blocking

We can implement time blocking to utilize our time more efficiently. To time block effectively, we need to ask ourselves a few quick questions:

- When do you have the most energy: morning, midday, or night?
- When are you in the best mood: morning, midday, or night?
- When do you feel the most productive: morning, midday, or night?

Once you discover when you feel the best, you can plan your time for optimal efficiency. For example, if you have the most energy and feel the most productive in the morning, you should time block your most challenging tasks during the first part of the day. If your energy is highest at night, that might be the best time to sit down and hone in on challenging tasks that require your utmost attention.

Look at your priorities from Quadrants 1 and 2 of the Eisenhower Box. Thinking about the most challenging tasks, go ahead and time block them according to when you can concentrate on them best. While a standard to-do list is great, it doesn't tell you *when* the task will be done. That's where time blocking aids in efficiency and productivity in our lives.

It is important to note that you should not time block 100% of the hours available in your day. If you aim to time block about 75% of your free time, you will still have some time left for tasks that take longer than anticipated or for things you didn't expect. This strategy alleviates rush and undesired stress.

The Two-Minute Rule

Finally, it's time to implement the two-minute rule to further increase our productivity on the high seas! Fortunately, this efficiency technique is relatively basic. It says that if you can do it in two minutes, you should do it the minute the task appears!

We can use the two-minute rule in two unique ways. First, the two-minute rule is suitable for those tasks we can easily put off, but that need to be done. For example, think about what happens when you check the mail. Getting a mail pile that stacks up throughout the week is easy. Instead, the two-minute rule says, "Just sort the mail when you first get it!" Toss junk mail in the trash and take care of any necessary bills. Once it's done, it's done! If it never piles up, it ceases to feel like a massive chore at the end of the week.

We can also use the two-minute rule when it's time to start a significant task. Sometimes, tasks seem so big that we don't know where to start. So, we don't. We procrastinate until we put ourselves under extreme pressure to produce results. The two-minute rule says we can kick off momentum for more significant projects by completing big tasks in smaller chunks - two minutes at a time!

Let's say you have a long history report to write. It seems so daunting that you don't even want to start. But you go ahead and format your paper. Then, you write the title page. Next, you format the introductory paragraph. Soon, your paper is in full swing.

The two-minute rule kicked you off, and now you're on a roll!

Only some efficiency techniques will be for everyone, and you might find that different methods work for you at different times. Give each one a shot and determine which tools are for you. Productivity is as personal to you as your unique personality, mate!

KEEPING PROCRASTINATION AT BAY

Despite the tips and tricks and productivity hacks we've discussed thus far, a word still lingers over our heads each day. Procrastination. It happens. It's part of the human experience.

People procrastinate for any number of reasons. We may dislike the task at hand. It's undesirable, and we don't want to do it. Sometimes, we procrastinate because we overestimate what we can achieve in a given timeframe. We may get discouraged and stop putting in the work. Other times, the sheer amount of tasks we have to complete leads us to paralysis. Instead of taking the bull by the horns, we get overwhelmed and do nothing. So, how do we keep pesky procrastination at bay?

First, as previously mentioned, we can break large tasks into smaller, more manageable steps. We can also make tedious tasks more enjoyable. Take cleaning your room as an example. You might have had a long week, and your room is in disarray. There are clothes everywhere, papers from school, and not a small amount of fast food containers. Not only do you despise cleaning your room, but you are also overwhelmed by the amount of cleaning needed.

Let's start by making the task more enjoyable. Do you like to listen to music? Is there a particular podcast you enjoy? Crank it up! You can instantaneously change your mood with just a little energy boost! Do you appreciate pleasant smells from a diffuser or have a favorite candle to burn? Use scents to create an environment you want to be in.

Now, break the chore of cleaning your entire room into smaller, more manageable parts. Start by tackling the trash and addressing the laundry on your floor and bed. Make your bed. Now part of your room is already clean! Follow that by clearing your desk and handling the papers accumulated throughout the week. Before your playlist is up, your room is essentially clean!

Still, when procrastination looms, getting started can be the hardest part. Try to do just one small task related to an overall project to build momentum, even if you don't have time to finish the entire chore. The Ziegarnik effect shows that any unfinished tasks create mental tension, making us more likely to want to finish them soon. The first step is often to begin!

MASTERING TIME MANAGEMENT: CREATING LIFE BALANCE

When we master our time, we create many advantages in our lives. We make better decisions and perform better at school and work. We gain responsibility and independence and create more time for those activities we love. When we balance our schedules, we find more time to relax and unwind with family and friends. We also reduce potential anxiety surrounding projects and deadlines.

The good news is that teens often have regular schedules. You likely go to school at specific times each day. Athletic practices typically occur about the same time. The youth group meets at the same time each week. It should be easy to build a study schedule around these regularly occurring events.

Remember that the first step is to write your schedule down. What to-dos are you tasked with this week? Consider academic and personal deadlines and events. Then, prioritize each task. You can use the Eisenhower Box to help. Once you understand your priorities, get them on a calendar. Use tools such as Google Calendar to map out your week. Then, start tackling your list. Use apps such as Forest or Remember the Milk, or try the Pomodoro Technique to support your focus and efficiency.

And what does our trusty Captain have to say? Let's find out! Let's Ask the Captain about his personal productivity hacks!

Ask the Captain: Time Management Hacks Revealed

Ask the Captain

Captain, why is time management so important for teens?

Ah, time management is the wind in your sails, young sailor! Just as a well-guided ship reaches its destination smoothly, managing your time ensures you can navigate life's rocky waters without getting lost in the storm! It helps you balance your studies, leisure, and responsibilities, reducing stress and boosting productivity.

What's one secret to efficient time management that works for you, Captain?

Arrr, me laddie! It's easy to get overwhelmed out here on the high seas, where much must be done. But remember, efficient time management isn't about cramming a bunch of tasks into every minute on board. It's about knowing when to do the work. If you're a morning person, hoist your productivity flag early and tackle your most challenging tasks. Find your wind and use it to your advantage, mate.

With so many things to do, how do you make sure your most important tasks get done?

Prioritizing my to-dos is essential to charting my appropriate daily course, lad. I must evaluate my task list based on what is important and urgent. Just like I have to address a looming storm before a minor squall, you also have to prioritize tasks with specific goals and deadlines. I use the Eisenhower Box as a trusty compass to help me keep my ship steered right!

> **My schedule is really overwhelming, but I still have trouble saying no to others, even if I don't want to do their ask. Can you help?**
>
> *"No" is a powerful word, lad. It is a necessary word to use when our ship is already full of cargo. Remember to decline with grace if someone invites you ashore when you should be at the helm of your studies. You can say, "I have other responsibilities right now." People who love you will understand. Always remember to protect your course. When you list your priorities and clearly see your obligations, saying no will become easier, too!*

> **I struggle to get started on tasks I don't want to do. How do I fend off the sirens of procrastination, Captain?**
>
> *Procrastination is the sea serpent of productivity, mate! To tame this wild beast, it's essential to understand why you might be delaying the task. Is it too big for you to manage at once? Break daunting jobs into smaller, more manageable bits. If a task is dull, add in a little spice! Do it with a friend or kick on a tune. Remember, the most challenging part is to begin. Set sail immediately, even if it is just a short voyage.*

> **Captain, how do I find balance in my life through time management? My schedule is really overwhelming sometimes.**
>
> *Balancing the ship of life can be a tricky task, lad. Map out your weekly voyage to understand how to use your time. Consider how much time you must allocate to your studies, leisure, family, and friends. Remember to stay flexible, and don't feel the need to schedule every minute of your day. Often, scheduling about 75% of our time is enough. Just like I need to adjust my sails based on the wind, leave some wiggle room for unexpected events and challenges that might arise for you each week. Remember, a balanced life will ensure you don't veer off course, even when the occasional storm may arise.*

Remember, sailors, time is your ship, and you are its only captain. Steer it well, and you will reach a treasure trove full of dreams. Let time drift away, however, and you may find yourself lost in the doldrums of the sea. The secret is planning, discipline, and having the courage to stay true to the right course for you. Set your sights on the horizon; favorable winds will guide your course!

The North Star's Guiding Light (Key Chapter Takeaways)

- Time is your most precious treasure. Unlike money, you can't get it back once it's spent. How you use your time determines the course of your life.
- Plan ahead to prevent losing control of your time. Prioritize tasks based on urgency and importance using the Eisenhower Box.
- Time management is more than filling every minute of your time with tasks. Simplify your work and complete tasks faster by aligning them with your natural energy rhythms.
- Learn to say no to tasks or requests that don't align with your priorities or when you are already overextended with your commitments.
- Consider tracking your time for a week to learn where your hours go. Modify and adjust your schedule accordingly.
- Use apps like Google Calendar, Forest, or Remember the Milk to help organize and track your most important to-dos.
- Explore time management methods, like the Pomodoro Technique, time blocking, and the two-minute rule, to enhance productivity.
- Overcome procrastination by breaking large tasks into smaller steps. Find ways to make them enjoyable, too!

10

SURFING THE DIGITAL WAVE: NAVIGATING ONLINE LIFE

We've navigated so much of life already together, am I right? We've sailed some calm waters and others have been more turbulent, but you are finding your sea legs on this grand adventure!

In this chapter, we have our sights set on the vast and ever-changing digital ocean, where understanding how to navigate effectively is critical for your well-being, safety, and productivity both on land and at sea. Just as sailors must master the sea's winds and tides, you must also master the currents of online life. So, let's batten down the hatches and set sail into the digital realm!

THE CYBER HEALTH EQUATION: BALANCING SCREEN TIME

As sailors, we all know the importance of balance, both on and off the ship! The same principle applies to the digital world. Too much screen time, and we run the risk of capsizing!

Too much screen time plays a role in both our physical and mental health. Overexposure to screens can lead to eye strain, sleep disturbances, and anxiety. Like too much time at sea can leave a sailor weary, too much screen time depletes our bodies of renewal processes. Thus, we need to set limits on our daily media use to protect the health of our vessels.

What are some ways to limit our screen time? First, we can consider daily digital detoxes. Set a specific time each day when you put your screens down for at least an hour. I suggest you do this before bed, too. Many people dedicate a whole day at the end of the week to unplug; some even take a week off at the end of every month. Find a digital detox practice that works for you to give your mind time to unplug entirely.

It is also essential to engage in offline hobbies, much like exploring a new island you encounter at sea. Read a book, play a sport, or engage in creative activities. These hobbies provide a break from the screen, build new skills, and nurture a spirit of relaxation. Just as sailors acquire new skills at each port of call, you can enrich your life through diversifying your offline experiences.

DIGITAL WAVES: NAVIGATING SOCIAL MEDIA AND ONLINE SAFETY

Sailing through the vast world of digital and social media can be exciting. Still, it's essential to recognize the potential pitfalls hidden within the endless waves of information. Just as a sailor stays alert for unexpected challenges at sea, you must be vigilant in the online realm.

Think of your personal information as treasure you've stashed on your digital island. Please keep it safe! Refrain from broadcasting details like your full name, home address, or phone number on social media platforms. Dive into the privacy settings of the websites and apps you frequent, adjusting them to ensure only trusted mates can view your data.

However, even in this digital sea, pirates are on the prowl. Online scammers skilled in deception are always looking for unsuspecting users. It's crucial to be discerning: don't trust every friendly flag you see. Avoid sharing personal details or sending doubloons (or money) to strangers, even if they appear legitimate.

Lastly, consider your passwords as the anchors keeping your digital ship secure. Craft solid and unique codes, combining letters, numbers, and symbols. Update them frequently, ensuring no unauthorized buccaneers can access your prized digital possessions.

In this vast digital ocean, your best compass is awareness. Keep it by your side, and you'll always find safe shores in the online world.

NAVIGATING THE POWER OF AI

As we delve deeper into the digital ocean, AI, or artificial intelligence, is becoming a staple in our daily lives. From social media algorithms to voice assistants, AI is everywhere. But while these tools offer incredible features and convenience, navigating this landscape with awareness is essential. Here are some necessary things to consider as it pertains to AI in our lives:

- **Know AI's Limits.** AI isn't magic. It makes decisions based on data it's been fed. Sometimes, it can get things wrong or provide results that don't make sense. Always double-check, and don't assume AI is always right.
- **Guard Your Privacy.** Many of our favorite apps and platforms use AI to enhance our experience. However, they might also collect and analyze vast amounts of our data. Always check app permissions and be cautious about sharing personal details. Your digital privacy matters!
- **Watch Out for Bias**. AI tools can sometimes reflect or exaggerate societal biases, especially if trained using skewed data. Remember to think critically and know that AI isn't always entirely impartial.
- **AI Isn't a Replacement.** While it's tempting to let AI tools handle everything, remember they're tools, not replacements for human skills or judgment. Combining AI's capabilities with your unique human touch is always a good idea.

- **How AI Thinks.** Not all AI tools openly share how they make decisions. In certain situations, it's vital to understand why AI is making a particular recommendation, especially if it affects important choices in your life.
- **The Job Landscape.** AI is changing how many industries operate, impacting future job opportunities. While this means some jobs might become less common, new ones will emerge. It's always good to stay informed about how AI might shape your dream career.
- **Real or Fake.** AI can create hyper-realistic fake images, videos, and even voices. Quickly check before believing everything you see or hear, especially online. In the age of AI, a healthy dose of skepticism can go a long way.
- **Stay Safe.** Like you wouldn't download a suspicious app on your phone, be cautious about which AI tools you use. Ensure they come from reputable sources and don't pose security risks.
- **Think before You AI.** Always consider the ethical side of using AI. Just because an app can predict something or makes a report quicker to write doesn't always mean using it is the right choice. It's essential to balance convenience with morality.
- **Keep Learning** The world of AI is constantly evolving. Stay curious and updated. The more you understand AI, the better equipped you'll be to use it in beneficial and safe ways.

In a nutshell, AI offers exciting possibilities and conveniences. Still, it's essential to approach it with a mix of enthusiasm and caution. By understanding its limitations and potential, you can maximize what AI offers while staying safe and informed.

DIGITAL CITIZENSHIP: RESPONSIBLE ONLINE BEHAVIOR

We know we must limit screen time and protect our identities online. But when we need to spend time on social media or the web, how do we behave in ways that represent ourselves well? We all know misbehaving can be easy when we can hide behind a screen!

A good rule of thumb for responsible online behavior is to treat people with the same respect online as you would in real life. Respect diverse viewpoints just as you would respect various creatures in the sea. There is room for an array of life on the ocean floor. Engage in discussions and disagreements constructively.

Also, remember that the digital ocean is permanent. Everything you post has a way of being found. Think before posting. Like a message in a bottle, what you post can drift back to you at inopportune and unexpected times.

Finally, be cautious of cyberbullying. If you encounter cyberbullying or witness it, report it to a trusted adult or the platform authorities, just like you would report a distress signal at sea. We have to protect each other. If you see something, say something to help protect the vulnerable and yourself.

NOURISHING REAL LIFE: BALANCING DIGITAL AND OFFLINE WORLDS

Although we have thus far concentrated on some of the adverse effects of technology in our lives, we also know that technology is a tool that helps us stay connected with family and friends. However, if we don't create limits to its use, we can harm our mental and physical health. If we spend too much time on our screens, we avoid exercise, creativity, new learning, and the art of play. These are all requirements for a well-balanced, fulfilling life.

Humans are designed for real-world connections and experiences. Spending time with people we know and love nurtures bonds and increases our interpersonal skills. Suppose we avoid these experiences by scrolling social media, gaming, and video sharing. In that case, we are less likely to be happy, healthy individuals.

Create some rules around your screen time to promote healthy social media use. You can create boundaries around when and where it is appropriate to use your device. For example, if your phone keeps you up at night, consider charging it outside your bedroom, such as on the kitchen counter. Creating this boundary can promote higher-quality rest.

You can also set a timer to limit the time you allow yourself to scroll aimlessly. Get up and move when the timer ends. If you are playing a game, make yourself get up when you reach the next level. Creating physical movement in your life promotes good physical health and increased mental well-being.

Finally, remember that your real-life responsibilities should precede any social media use. Look at your to-do list before you start to scroll mindlessly. Use tools previously mentioned in this book, such as Google Calendar, to organize your weekly priorities. They will help you manage your time efficiently, like a compass guiding a ship at sea.

Remember, in the vast ocean of technology, your best asset is a combination of knowledge and critical thinking. Embrace the future, but always with awareness!

And now, let's Ask the Captain our lingering questions about navigating the digital seas!

Ask the Captain: Navigating the Digital Seas

Ask the Captain

Captain, the digital world seems overwhelming when I think about it sometimes. There is so much that can go wrong - it stresses me out! How can I ensure my safety and privacy online?

Ahoy, mate! That's an important question you ask. The digital seas can undoubtedly feel overwhelming at times. First, limit your time online for optimal mental and physical health. Setting boundaries with our technology can be the first step in being safe. There are other things you can do to safeguard your presence online. Guard your personal information, such as your name, birthdate, and address. Don't forget to update your passwords regularly. Also, be cautious of online scams. Never give money to someone you don't know.

Captain, I hear a lot about online bullying and harassment. What should I do if I witness such behavior?

Aye, cyberbullying is a real menace in today's world, shipmate. Suppose you encounter it yourself or witness someone being harassed. In that case, you should always report the event to a trusted adult and the relevant platform authorities. Just as you would look out for a friend in real life, you must also look out for people in the virtual world.

It's just so easy for me to get sucked into my phone. There is so much to see and do online - I can go down a rabbit hole pretty fast! How do I balance screen time and being present in real life?

Ahoy, mate! Balancing screen time is like finding an equilibrium between work and leisure on a ship. We need to dedicate time to both online and offline activities. Make a list of activities you enjoy doing offline, including spending time with family and friends. Then, ensure you are working on those pastimes and hobbies daily. You will feel more well-rounded and energized by your time in the digital world.

Captain, I am a little concerned about some things I posted in the past. What should I consider before posting in the future?

That's an excellent question, mate! Posting online can be problematic because we know that even if we delete a post in the future, there is permanence on the internet overall. Before posting, always consider whether you are sharing something you would be comfortable with everyone seeing now and in the future. Just as sailors leave footprints on the shore, your digital trail can have lasting consequences.

As we navigate the digital sea, know that the tide will ebb and flow. Some days we will go down a social media rabbit hole, and other days greater balance will prevail. Don't get discouraged if some days are harder than others. It's never too late to rebalance and begin again.

The North Star's Guiding Light (Key Chapter Takeaways)

- Overexposure to screens can lead to physical and mental health concerns, making it critical to set limits on daily media use.
- Regular digital detoxes are like mini vacations for the mind. They allow you to unplug from digital devices for a few hours or a full day each week.
- Offline hobbies, such as reading, playing sports, or pursuing creative experiences, not only provide breaks from screens but also contribute to our rest and rejuvenation.
- Protect your online privacy at all costs. Avoid sharing personal information and use privacy settings to control who can access your profiles and accounts.
- Ensure your passwords are secure by regularly updating your accounts with unique combinations of letters, numbers, and symbols.
- Engage in online dialogue the same way you would in real life. Treat others with respect, and remember that anything you type is permanent. If you experience or witness cyberbullying, report it to the platform authorities or trusted adults.
- Create boundaries for your screen time to prioritize real-world connections with family and friends.
- Use tools like Google Calendar to organize your weekly priorities and manage your time efficiently. Setting boundaries for when to use your digital devices can promote higher-quality rest and a healthier life balance.

11

CHARTING YOUR PATH: PLANNING YOUR CAREER AND HUNTING FOR JOBS

As we wrap up our voyage on the high seas, it's time to start charting our course towards the future - including a thriving career! To navigate these uncharted waters, we must embark on self-discovery, career exploration, and professional development to ensure a prosperous journey into our future lives. Let's set our sights on the horizon and navigate this critical last chapter toward a career that aligns with our purpose and, hopefully, our passion, too!

SELF-EXPLORATION: IDENTIFYING YOUR INTERESTS AND SKILLS

A critical first step in the pathway toward our future is, quite simply, knowing ourselves! Who are you, and what do you like? What are your passions and interests? Where does your true purpose lie?

These can be big questions, so let's take a moment to break them down.

To find your true purpose, thinking about three different areas of your life is often helpful. First, make a list of your skills and strengths. Where do you excel naturally in the world? Are you good with words? Do you have a knack for numbers? Are you artistic or musically inclined? When we take a moment to identify what we're good at, it can help clarify various careers that could align with our natural skills.

Next, what do you love to do? Are you social by nature or perhaps a bit more of an introvert? Do you like to spend time alone, or do you prefer to work as part of a team? Do you have any hobbies or interests that you absolutely love? What would you do if you could do anything in your free time? Who doesn't want a career that aligns with what we enjoy doing each day?

Finally, what does the world need? What keeps you up at night about the world in which we live? Is there a cause you are passionate about? Where in your community are you currently engaged? When we think about how the world is suffering, we can often identify a path toward a purpose-filled life.

Now, place your lists into a Venn diagram with a circle in the middle of where the other three circles intersect. This middle circle is where you find your purpose. When you look at your skills, passions, and the world's needs, you can start to see a path formulated right before you. Be open to what you see here. You might be surprised at what begins to surface as you do this self-work.

Now that you have determined your dharma or purpose let's look at some career exploration opportunities to further define your next steps toward your future.

CAREER EXPLORATION: UNDERSTANDING DIFFERENT CAREER PATHS

There are so many new and evolving careers that knowing where to start on the career exploration path can seem overwhelming. The world of employment is like a vast ocean - the possibilities are seemingly endless! As sea captains explore different routes and destinations, we must also navigate the various career paths. Here are a few suggestions for getting started on such an overwhelming task:

- **Plot Your Course**. Research different careers and industries. Understand their demands, opportunities, and challenges. If it is helpful, make a list of pros and cons for each one. For example, is salary more important than your skillset being appropriately utilized? Do you want to work from home or be in the office daily? Do you prefer to travel, or is a nine-to-five job more your speed? You will see clear courses unfold by clarifying the opportunities and challenges of various positions.
- **Mentorship Matter.**: Seek guidance from experienced professionals who can share their insights and experiences. If you are considering becoming a teacher, interview a few of your own! Interested in the realm of finance? Ask your parents for a trusty advisor you

could turn to for more advice. Don't be afraid to ask honest questions. Employees within the industry have a lot of insight they can share.

- **Engage in Experiential Learning.** There are so many ways we can explore different career paths in a hands-on learning environment. Here are a few ways you can gain first-hand experience in potential career fields:

- **Job Shadowing.** As mentioned briefly, when you know someone in a particular field of interest, you should be bold and open to their mentorship and experience. Beyond simply interviewing them about their job, consider asking to shadow them for a day. Job shadowing is just watching someone do their job and can give you an idea of what a typical day looks like. By the end of the day, you will have a good feel about whether that line of work is right for you!

- **Service Learning.** Service learning opportunities are designed to help you engage in your community through projects centered around real-world, complex issues. These projects allow you to learn about issues present in our society, such as hunger and homelessness, poverty, pollution, and more. You may find a niche you have yet to realize interested you through giving back to your community in a positive way.

- **Internships.** Internships allow learning about careers while gaining real-world work experience over an extended amount of time. Some internships will be paid, while others are not. They provide hands-on opportunities for learning the intricacies of a job before committing to that career pathway more permanently.

Whichever exploratory pathway you choose to take, you have several options. Choose the option that is accessible to you and that makes sense based on your passion and purpose. There is no right or wrong way to explore future careers. The more diverse experiences you give yourself now, the more confident you will be with your decision in the future.

CRAFTING YOUR RESUME: MAKING A STRONG FIRST IMPRESSION

So, you've gone down the rabbit hole of career exploration. You have identified your strengths and skill set, passions, and purpose. Then, you've sought opportunities to learn more about potential career pathways that align with your goals. Now, it's time to maximize your chances at various options within your field of interest. But how do you make that first impression count?

Your resume is like a flag flying high on the mast of your ship, signaling your qualifications and abilities to future employers or volunteer entities. Like flags communicate a ship's identity, your resume introduces you to the professional world.

Think of your resume as a way to tell your professional story. You will want to highlight your skills, experiences, and achievements so that your future employer gains confidence in how you align with the job requirements. In this way, you will want to tailor your resume for each job application you submit.

Here are a few essential tips to start:

- **Use a resume template.** Plenty are free through Canva or by conducting a Google search. Make it easy on yourself and choose a template that already exists!
- **Create subheadings for clarity.** If you use a template, subheadings will likely already be outlined. If not, here are a few to include: *Summary, Education, Experience,* and *Skills.*
- **Craft a strong summary.** Underneath your name and contact information, the first part of your resume typically involves a catchphrase that highlights who you are. Your words should be brief, clear, and relevant. A summary is usually, at most, three or four lines of text. State why you are the one for the position based on your experience and skills.
- **Highlight your education.** Although you may only have high school experience, include as much detail as possible about your academic career. Your GPA, relevant coursework (such as AP or CTE courses), and any awards can all be included in this section to highlight your potential and skills.
- **Sell your experiences.** Sure, you may yet to have an official part-time job, but you still have life experiences related to your desired position or opportunity. Babysitting and pet watching are excellent to highlight, as they demonstrate your reliability, sense of responsibility, and communication skills! If you are involved in clubs, extracurriculars, or athletics, include those experiences here, too!

- **Tailor your skills to the job description.** Is the company seeking special technology skills, knowledge of a second language, or other traits you possess? Emphasize these job-specific skills in the final section of your resume. You will stand out as an individual aligned with the company's needs.
- **Polish your resume.** Be sure to review your resume carefully when all is said and done. Many eyes to proof and edit your work will be helpful to you here. Your family and friends may even think of a skill or experience you possess that you didn't include. Look for spelling and grammatical errors, too!

PREPARING FOR JOB INTERVIEWS: SHOWCASING YOUR SKILLS AND ENTHUSIASM

You've determined your purpose and passion. You've found a few different careers that align with your goals. Your resume is polished and aligned to the job you desire. And now, the dreaded interview arrives! How do you sell yourself in an atmosphere where you can no longer hide behind a paper resume or a screen?

Although intimidating, a job interview is just an opportunity to showcase your skills, knowledge, and enthusiasm. What's easier than talking about yourself? Here are some additional tips and tricks to ensure you meet success:

- **Research the job and the company.** This is one of the key areas where many potential employees need to improve. Research the company's vision, mission, and history to understand its trajectory and current goals. Include some of what you learn in the interview to show interest in their needs and how you can support them with your knowledge and expertise.

- **Determine questions to ask.** After your research, create two to three questions about the company or your position. This demonstrates further curiosity and interest in where the company is going and where they've already been.

- **Practice makes perfect.** Just as sailors at sea rehearse different drills for rocky seas, we also need to practice in preparation for our interview. Start by using artificial intelligence tools or a Google search to research common interview questions based on the job you are applying for. Practice your writing and speaking responses to gain confidence in answering each one. Even better? Get feedback from a trusted adult.

- **Dress for success.** Dress appropriately for the interview based on the type of work you are applying for. Dressing professionally shows respect for the opportunity. Keep jewelry to a minimum and avoid any articles of clothing that may seem tattered or worn.

- **Showcase your strengths.** Discuss your skills and experiences with confidence. Be enthusiastic about the position and how your knowledge aligns with the opportunity.

When you finish the interview, don't forget to send a follow-up communication to the hiring team. Whether it is an email or a handwritten note, this simple gesture goes a long way to show your enthusiasm and interest in the opportunity at stake.

UNDERSTANDING WORKPLACE ETIQUETTE: NAVIGATING YOUR FIRST JOB

When you finally land your desired position, you will likely experience some stress. Your first job is like setting sail on your maiden voyage at sea. It's an exciting time but can require extra attention to navigate those first few weeks.

To help you adjust to the new opportunity, first, don't be afraid to ask for some cooperation from the crew! You will likely work closely with the hiring manager as you train and transition. Be friendly, open to learning, and ask lots of questions. Teamwork will be vital even as you become increasingly independent in your work.

You will likely make mistakes during these first few weeks. Whether you miscount money or forget a closing task, know that mistakes will happen, and it's the learning that matters most in the end. Learn from your experiences, apologize for your mistakes, and adjust as you go. Your manager will remember what it's like to be new. Show that you are open to adapting as you learn more about the scope of your job.

Finally, treat your workplace with respect and professionalism at all times. Just like a captain takes pride in maintaining his ship, take pride in your work environment. Keep your environment clean and tidy, and continually review checklists to ensure all to-do items are complete. Please don't leave until your work is finished or it is time to clock out from your shift.

And now, it's our last opportunity to talk to our beloved captain! Let's see what he says about life in the working world!

Ask the Captain: Your Workplace Questions Revealed

Ask the Captain

Captain, I'm ready to apply for my first job. What are some important skills and qualities I should develop as I prepare?
Ahoy, young lad! It's excellent that you are preparing for your first shot at a job! There are lots of general skills you can focus on developing that are necessary for almost any job you land. Consider building skills such as time management, communication, and problem-solving to be well-rounded. Additionally, qualities such as responsibility, punctuality, and a strong work ethic are highly valued by employers. Consider how to highlight those skills on your resume and in your interview.

What types of jobs are suitable for teens who are just starting their working careers?
There are a variety of entry-level jobs that are typically suitable for teens. Think about jobs in retail sales, food service, or babysitting. These positions are usually flexible with teens' schedules as they balance work and school.

Captain, what are some good ways to find jobs in the local area? I'm not sure where to start.

There are a lot of ways we can search for jobs in our local communities. Opportunities are all around! You can look through online job boards, check out local newspaper ads, and even visit local businesses in person to see who has Now Hiring ads. Don't forget about sharing your job search with family and friends. They may have potential leads, too!

I hear there may be specific rules or guidelines teens should follow regarding work hours and safety for younger personnel. What do I need to know?

You aren't wrong here, mate! There are laws and regulations for teen workers that vary by location. Teens should be aware of work hour limitations, restrictions on hazardous tasks, and minimum wage requirements in your area. These regulations are designed to protect your overall health and well-being on the job.

How can I maximize my ability to make a good impression on my job interview, even if it is my very first job?

They always say there is no second chance to make an excellent first impression, right, mate? This is especially true in a job interview. Research the company, practice common interview questions, dress professionally, and always arrive slightly ahead of time. During the interview, don't forget to maintain good eye contact, speak clearly, and express enthusiasm for the job.

Captain, I am ready for my first job, but I am worried about my work-life balance. I have a lot on my plate. What do you suggest?

Time management is vital when you're looking to secure your first job, lad. First, create a schedule that allocates your time for work, school, homework, extracurricular activities, and personal time. You have to design a plan that works for you. Use apps to help you stay organized if necessary. Also, don't hesitate to communicate your availability and limitations to your employer. The more transparent you are upfront, the easier it is to maintain a work-life balance.

Captain, what are the benefits of having a part-time job? Does it really matter that much?

While only you can decide if a part-time job is right for you, several benefits stem from employment during the teenage years. A job will help you develop essential life skills, gain financial independence, and learn the value of money. It can also provide a sense of responsibility and help you explore potential careers.

> **Captain, what advice do you have for teens who want to make the most of their first job experience?**
>
> Teens should approach their first job with a positive attitude, a willingness to learn, and a commitment to hard work. They should seek opportunities for skill development and always be professional.

As you embark on your career journey, remember that every sea captain was once a novice sailor simply riding the waves. With self-discovery, career exploration, a well-crafted resume, and appropriate interview prep, you will quickly be sailing on the seas of success. It will take no time before you become the captain of your professional destiny. Hoist your career flag high and be prepared to ride the waves of the journey. It is sure to be an amazing ride!

The North Star's Guiding Light (Key Chapter Takeaways)

- Self-discovery is the first step toward a successful career journey. Identify your strengths, passions, and the world's needs to find your true purpose.
- Research different careers and consider their demands, opportunities, and challenges. Engage in experiential learning opportunities like job shadowing and internships to learn more about different career pathways.
- Create a resume that makes a solid professional introduction to who you are. Include a summary highlighting your assets, and expand upon your education, experience, and skills.
- Prepare for a job interview by researching the company in advance. Practice common interview questions and seek feedback to gain confidence.
- Always send follow-up information after the interview to express continued interest in the job.

Help a Fellow Sailor Out!

As you continue on your voyage, you can help to set the sail for other people like you.

Simply by sharing your honest opinion of this book and a little about your own experience, you'll help other teenagers to find the essential advice they're looking for.

Thank you so much for your support. Now, set sail, and enjoy the view!

Scan the QR code to leave a review!

CONCLUSION

Mastering life skills during the teenage years sets us up for a smoother transition to adulthood. Each skill discussed in this book will equip you with the confidence and capability to handle various life situations and prepare you for future success. A brief summary of these skills is provided here:

- **Navigating Independence:** Mastering basic life skills, such as understanding financial literacy and initiating early career planning, sets us up to become increasingly more independent as we enter adulthood.
- **Building Relationships and Communication Skills:** Cultivating healthy relationships and honing effective communication skills equips us for better interpersonal interactions with people in our everyday lives.
- **Decision-Making and Problem-Solving Skills:** Informed decision-making and effective problem-

solving techniques help us navigate complex situations with increased confidence and ease.

- **Health and Wellness:** Maintaining physical health, prioritizing mental well-being, and practicing digital wellness all impact the overall quality of our lives.

Now that you have these skills, it's time to start the journey of implementing them into your daily routines. Start small. Building good habits takes time. Choose one or two skills that will have the most impact on your life, given what you are facing today. Then, commit to one small change you can incorporate each day that will drive you toward the bigger change you want. The small change can be as simple as putting down your phone for just ten minutes before bed or drinking a glass of water right when you wake up. Even the tiniest of changes can eventually pack a big punch in our lives.

The power to change your life is always emboldened by the actions of the brave. As you journey towards a fulfilling and inspiring adulthood, know that everything you have read in this book is meant to equip you with the skills you need along the journey. At this point, all you need to do is simply begin. There will be mistakes and setbacks along your course. When you find yourself in those moments, know there is nothing wrong with beginning again. Sometimes, our journey must begin several times before we find ourselves on the appropriate course.

It is my hope that this book will continue to be a helpful guide in these critical years to follow. Depend on and reference it as often as you need. With this guidance, may you step into the adult world with all the confidence and competence a strong sailor can muster. As you set sail on the seas of your life, know that somewhere, I will always be rooting for you.

REFERENCES

No Ordinary Moments Nutrition. (n.d.). 15 Actionable Tips to be More Productive and Less Overwhelmed. https://www.noordinarymoments.co/blogs/news/15-actionable-tips-to-be-more-productive-and-less-overwhelmed

Apraku Psychiatry. (n.d.). Blog. https://www.apraku.com/feed/toxic-positivity

Centers for Disease Control and Prevention. National Center for Injury Prevention and Control. (2005). Choose respect community action kit: Helping preteens and teens build healthy relationships. http://www.aldine.k12.tx.us/cms/file_process/download.cfm?docID=BED9BF514B2EAD07

Evans, O. (2023, June 13). Primary and Secondary Emotions: Recognizing the Difference. Simply Psychology. https://www.simplypsychology.org/primary-and-secondary-emotions.html

Rich, T. (n.d.). Primary and Secondary Emotions. Richer Life Counseling. https://richerlifecounseling.com/primary-and-secondary-emotions/#:

TOP 25 LIGHTHOUSE QUOTES (of 96). A-Z Quotes. Accessed October 25, 2023. https://www.azquotes.com/quotes/topics/lighthouse.html

Tsai, J. (n.d.). Culture and Emotion. NOBA. https://nobaproject.com/modules/culture-and-emotion

Natural Solutions. (2023, June 1). HOW TO CUT BACK OR avoid sugar, 232, 4.

The Hearing Review (Online). (2017, April 26). The National Academies of Sciences, Engineering, and Medicine to Hold Dissemination Meeting June 9. n/a.

We Level Up. (n.d.). What Is Clinical Depression? Causes, Symptoms & Treatment. https://welevelup.com/treatment/clinical-depression/

Aquiestu Veayer. (n.d.). How to Do Laundry - How to Wash Clothes Step-by-Step. https://aquiestuveayer.com/how-to-do-laundry-how-to-wash-clothes-step-by-step.html

GradSchoolHub. (n.d.). 5 Study Tips For Graduate Students. https://www.gradschoolhub.com/resources/5-study-tips-for-graduate-students/

Unito. (n.d.). How to Prioritize: Getting Your Important Work Done. https://unito.io/blog/how-to-prioritize/